WRITING
BEHAVIORAL
OBJECTIVES

WRITING BEHAVIORAL OBJECTIVES
a new approach

H. H. McAshan, Director
Project Ideals
College of Education
University of Florida
Gainesville, Florida

Harper & Row, Publishers
New York, Evanston, and London

The education of my
two very fine children,
Brian and Beth, in whom
both parents are well pleased

WRITING BEHAVIORAL OBJECTIVES: a new approach
Copyright © 1970 by H. H. McAshan

LIBRARY OF CONGRESS CATALOG CARD NUMBER: 78-118232

CONTENTS

Over the years, educators have been stating their goals in very general terms. For them, this has been an acceptable procedure because it allowed considerable freedom in developing a program and planning activities. However, it was difficult to develop evaluative techniques that could measure satisfactorily the degree to which these goals were realized. Yielding to the pressures from many sources to be more precise in statements of goals and to determine more accurately how effective our educational programs are, educators have turned to the development of more specific objectives. These are usually referred to as behavioral objectives, performance objectives, or other terms that indicate a higher degree of specificity. This step has made it easier to develop evaluative techniques.

Dr. H. H. McAshan has had unusual success in helping teachers develop behavioral objectives derived from specific goals for their educational programs. In his initial effort, he prepared a bulletin that was published by the Florida Educational Research and Development Council on "Writing Behavioral Objectives." This publication has gone through three separate printings and has been widely used in the State of Florida. Moreover, Dr. McAshan has conducted workshops for teachers in Florida which have been eminently successful in helping them to understand the concept of writing both behavioral and other types of performance objectives. With this experience as a background, he is well qualified to prepare this text on writing behavioral objectives for curriculum development. It should be of particular value for the training of college students and for school people interested in being more specific in stating their educational goals and evaluating their outcomes.

J. B. White

Executive Secretary
Florida Educational Research
and Development Council

Writing Behavioral Objectives: A New Approach is intended to help meet the specific needs of college-level students who are preparing for future employment in education or other behavioral science areas and for teachers, researchers, and curriculum program planners who need to improve both the planning and evaluation of their own professional responsibilities.

This book deals with the techniques or mechanics of writing behavioral and other types of performance objectives using a goals approach. Techniques are developed that are designed to promote objective writing competency in both the instructional and noninstructional areas. A second book is being prepared that proposes to help the learner increase his skill in writing objectives in the affective, psychomotor, and higher behavioral levels of the cognitive domain.

The text does not assume any background in teaching, in curriculum development, or in the writing of behavioral objectives. The entire body of information contained in the text has been planned to present the desired specifics in a direct and precise manner. Several learning strategies usually associated with programmed instruction have been incorporated into this text as follows: (1) The text is highly organized into a sequential format so that it can be utilized to teach both large and small groups. (2) Each chapter has its own specific objectives and evaluation measure stated at its beginning to serve as a study and evaluation guide for the reader. (3) All major concepts are reinforced throughout the text; an example is that ideas introduced in Chapter 2 are thoroughly taught in Chapters 3 and 4, and reviewed as a total process in Chapter 5. (4) The text is self-sustaining as a program for individual study or for utilization in a workshop situation. (5) Learner incentive and morale are built into the text through the utilization of objectives and tests that should provide many success experiences. Beginning with Chapter 1, the objectives require only simple memory type of knowledge, but gradually develop into some higher cognitive levels of understanding throughout the later chapters.

The types of performance objectives developed in the text are broken into three groups: specific noninstructional, minimum level behavioral, and desired level behavioral. Emphasis is placed upon the development of skills in writing objectives at the desired behavioral level.

A preliminary draft of this manuscript was published by the Florida Educational Research and Development Council and distributed to over 2000 educators in August 1969. By November 1969, the Council had received purchase orders for an additional 26,000 copies, which will attest to the value of this material in training people to write either performance or behavioral objectives.

H. H. McAshan

ACKNOWLEDGMENTS

The author wishes to express his sincere appreciation to Dr. Anita J. Harrow, whose workshops on Writing Behavioral Objectives utilizing the techniques described in this book have contributed much to the field testing of this material. In addition the author is in debt to Dr. Harrow for several meaningful suggestions which were found to be useful in the preparation of this final document.

The writer also desires to express his gratitude to Dr. J. B. White, Executive Secretary of the Florida Educational Research and Development Council, for his encouragement and decision to publish the original version of this text entitled "Writing Behavioral Objectives." This F.E.R.D.C. bulletin enabled the author to field test the material with approximately 30,000 teachers.

To the many teachers and administrators in the State of Florida who acted as subjects in field testing both the preliminary material and in the development of sample behavioral objectives through workshop experiences, the writer wishes to extend his thanks for their invaluable cooperation.

Chapter 1

INTRODUCTION

A place for everything, everything in its place.
—Franklin

Set all things in their own peculiar place, and
know that order is the greatest grace.
—Dryden

OBJECTIVE

The objective of this chapter is to develop in the reader a simple, basic knowledge of the rationale, general literature, and special considerations that are important in understanding and writing behavioral objectives. Proof that this goal has been accomplished will be established by the reader scoring at least 80 percent correct answers on the written or oral examination that follows.

1. Quality education refers to the effectiveness of any educational program in meeting its own _____ _____.

2. The primary reasons for the current emphasis upon writing behavioral objectives are to:

   (a)
   (b)
   (c)

3. Objectives intended to produce changes in learner behaviors are referred to as _____ _____.

4. Performance objectives that are nonlearner-oriented are
    called _____ _____ _____ .

5. According to the general literature, behavioral objectives
    can be effective when utilized:
    (a)
    (b)
    (c)
    (d)

6. Behavioral objectives should always be written at
    the _____ _____ .

7. Research will undoubtedly support the value of using
    behavioral objectives for purposes of _____ .

8. _____ should not be included in the statement
    of behavioral objectives.

9. Writing behavioral objectives at the desired level
    requires _____ _____ and
    considerable _____ _____ _____ .

10. Which of the two behavioral objective components, goals or
    behavioral evaluation activities, are most apt to remain
    fairly constant or stable? _____ .

(Answers to objective questions follow immediately after the
bibliography at the end of the book.)

RATIONALE

*Quality education refers to the effectiveness of any educational program
in meeting its own specifically defined objectives.* Individual teachers,
schools, and school systems may differ widely in the quality of their
instructional programs due to many variables. The realization that differences can and do exist makes it seem imperative that detailed study
of factors relating to quality assessment be undertaken in every school
program, and that methods for better evaluating quality be substantially
improved.

*The primary reasons for the current emphasis upon writing be-
havioral objectives are to: (1) aid in curriculum planning, (2) promote
increased pupil achievement, and (3) improve the techniques and skills
of program evaluation.* All phases of education, including both the instructional and noninstructional areas, are subject to study, evaluation,
and revision for improvement. Each area has its own unique problems
and objectives, but the processes utilized for study and evaluation can

be essentially the same. These processes include stating objectives based upon the observed needs, designing activities to bring about the necessary improvement, and then evaluating the results. With reference to the statement of objectives, *those that are intended to bring about changes in learner behaviors can be referred to as behavioral objectives; whereas, those performance objectives that are nonlearner-oriented may be called specific noninstructional objectives.*

Any worthwhile study concerned with educational program improvement must include the proper identification and description of specific objectives if the program variables are to be evaluated. Unless the specific objectives unique to each content area or educational project are clearly stated, the student, teacher, researcher, or program planner will not know what to do, how to do it, or when the goal has been accomplished.

Instructional program development and research usually begins with a specified need or an observable problem. These needs may begin with a teacher's observation of some overt behavior displayed by one or more students or from information obtained through various student testing programs. State Accreditation Standards may serve as prescribed needs from which objectives can be developed. Course content and sequence, along with subject area skill continuums, may be the basis for determining the needs. In any event, it is from these needs and problems that behavioral objectives are identified and form the basis for the major portion of all evaluation.

THE GENERAL LITERATURE

Anderson (1967) brought out the relationship between the objectives of an instructional program and the program's evaluation when he wrote, "Without well-stated objectives there is no basis for making any judgment as to whether or not the program has achieved the desired goals." Brothers and Holsclaw (1969), writing specifically for the subject area of spelling, suggest that the use of behavioral objectives has implications for training students in ways of acting and reacting in their particular subject area situations. Mayor (1967), the Director of Education for the American Association for the Advancement of Science (AAAS), stated that "the importance of the behavioral objectives in 'Science—A Process Approach' cannot be overemphasized." Thus, the AAAS program is stated in behavioral objective terms for each day's lesson as well as for the entire course.

There are many other obvious advocates of the behavioral and performance objective movement. Garvey (1968) lists the what and why of behavioral objectives in an attempt to promote better understanding of them. Mager (1962) indicated that an instructor might not have to do much else if he would just provide each learner with a copy of the specific course objectives. Popham (1969), who has long been a recognized leader advocating the use of behavioral objectives for curriculum development and evaluation purposes, has now been instrumental in establishing an Instructional Objective Exchange at the Center for the Study of Evaluation in Los Angeles, California. Plowman (1968) indicates that educational objectives guide what the teacher does and exert great influence upon the students. He states: "The most important thing a teacher can do is to modify behavior in a positive direction. He can do this by defining, teaching to, and evaluating pupil progress and instruction in light of behavioral objectives."

Other writers have admitted there are many benefits to be derived in utilizing behavioral objectives for curriculum planning but have stated several reservations. Atkin (1968) indicated that (1) we probably don't know or can't identify many of our most important educational objectives, (2) demands for behavioral specification will cause certain types of highly desirable innovations to become hampered by early demands for behavioral statements, (3) early articualtion of behavioral objectives may limit the range of the curriculum developer, (4) considerable educational potential may be lost if the teacher's attention is focused so closely on the behavioral goals that complete coverage of the learning situation is not allowed or viewed in the right context, and (5) behavioral objectives may never relate to the teaching of values since they are not easily measured.

Rath (1968) suggests that the requirements of specificity being advanced by Mager, Popham, Walbesser, and certain other behavioral objective advocates are in direct conflict with the values of teachers. In brief, Rath's paper stated "that the specificity now being demanded of curriculum workers and teachers in the writing of behavioral objectives runs contrary to their values of humanism and intellectualism." Ojemann (1968) calls attention to the fact that behavior in "controlled motivation" situations and in "on-his-own" situations may be entirely different. In controlled situations, behavior may conform to teacher expectations, whereas in on-his-own situations behavior may better indicate personal feelings of the significance of the content studied.

Kapfer (1968) advances the idea that writing behavioral objectives may alienate many teachers. This alienation would result from the degree of specificity required in the writing process, particularly in areas where such specificity can result in unreal, impractical, or trivial objectives. Coffyn (1968) warns of the possibility of stating objectives in terms of learnings that are almost impossible to detect, let alone measure. Teachers find little relationship between this type of objective and the aims of an actual lesson in a roomful of students.

In summing up the general literature concerning the development and use of behavioral objectives, it is important to point out that even the critics of certain features of behavioral objectives are also quick to admit some of their advantages. *It appears that behavioral objectives can be effective when utilized in the classroom, for research, in proposal writing, or for curriculum development activities. Behavioral objectives should always be written at the appropriate level,* and the writers should not attempt to be more specific with references to criterion standards of evaluation than the identified goal prescribes. In other words, do not specify any behavioral outcome for which evaluation data will not be available or for which the data will be too suspect. Finally, it should be recognized that much knowledge and experience is yet to be gained in the use of behavioral and performance objectives. *Research will undoubtedly support the value of using behavioral objectives for purposes of evaluation.* Research on the usefulness and value of behavioral objectives for curriculum development purposes and to increase student learning is far from complete. Thus, educational program planners should proceed with due caution and provide adequate in-service training opportunities for all faculties involved in curriculum development strategies requiring the writing and use of behavioral and performance objectives.

SPECIAL CONSIDERATIONS FOR BEHAVIORAL OBJECTIVE WRITING

Specificity

Most learning research or instructional program development is complex, and the investigators may need to *break down the problem area into its component parts before it will become manageable. This requires intensive study of specific parts of a problem area while keeping the practical aspects of the greater problem area in mind.* (An example might be the breaking down of broad program goals into smaller components that may be stated in more specific terms.) A *hidden danger* connected with this process *is the possibility of trying to draw from the results generalizations that are broader than the component part studied.* However, most problems will not become researchable until they have been broken into specifics. A rule of thumb here is that knowing most of the truth about small, related problems is usually better than knowing many partial truths about much larger areas.

Number of objectives

A study may be devoted to the testing of one major behavioral objective, representing a large unit of work, a number of subsidiary or individual skill behavioral objectives, or both major and subsidiary behavioral objectives. When several behavioral objectives are used, each should be stated separately in order to anticipate the type of evaluation analysis that will be required. Thus, the outcomes of each behavioral objective can definitely be accepted or rejected, based upon its own merit.

Clarity

The clarity with which each behavioral objective is stated is of utmost importance. The significance of such clarification is that the objective must not only identify the goal and the specific evaluation processes, but also should enable the investigators of the problem area to write out the procedures they will use in carrying out the proposed project. *It is obvious that few, if any, behavioral objectives ever reach a state of perfection, but can be rewritten and improved indefinitely.*

Use of procedures

Frequently, students, teachers, and administrators are confused concerning the relationship between procedures and behavioral objectives. Actually, no confusion is necessary. *Behavioral objectives identify goals and describe desired outcomes or performances learners should have as a result of participation in an activity. Procedures usually describe the content, treatments, processes, activities, or sequence of events that will take place in carrying out the design and evaluation activities.* Since most studies provide a specific section designed for the explanation of the procedures, *there is little to be gained by trying to indicate them again as a part of the behavioral objectives.* In fact, much confusion may result by their use in the statement of objectives.

Instructional dangers
The basic idea behind school system staff personnel and teachers writing their own desired level objectives is good and can be beneficial for all parties concerned. There are, however, concealed dangers that could work to the disadvantage of both if they are not fully recognized in the beginning. These dangers consist, in part, of the following possibilities:

1. Students are all very different in learning, attitudinal, and other behavioral characteristics. Therefore, it may do real harm to them if the same behavioral objectives are applied to all students with no change in the criteria or standards upon which the objectives are based. This is obvious when examining the differences found in aptitude between slow and advanced groups of students.

2. Teachers also differ to some degree in self-concepts, concepts of teaching, subject matter competence, educational training and backgrounds, social adjustment to children, personality, and other characteristics. Teachers writing behavioral objectives for identical courses of study may develop entirely different goals and expected outcomes unless some steps are taken to ensure at least some level of uniformity. Whereas some differences are good, desirable, and to be expected, it is natural that some of the objectives may miss the mark completely. The normal curve for individual effort could very well illustrate this point.

3. Teacher differences include their talents to communicate and teach. Much flexibility in the use of teacher talent could be lost with too much standardization of course objectives and/or methods of presentation. In addition, it would be a mistake to adopt the objectives prepared by teachers as a sort of "bible" for instructional goals, particularly if this is done at the expense of other educational values that have not been included in the behavioral statements.

4. *Writing behavioral objectives at the desired level requires both technical knowledge and considerable subject matter competency.* For these reasons the best behavioral objectives in any content area will come through team writing of objectives by small groups of teachers with common interests and common instructional areas of concern.

Much in-service training time is necessary to teach school administrators, staff members, and teachers how to write objectives in their special areas. This also requires time for cooperative planning. Without the in-service training and cooperative planning time, the results obtained by the teaching teams may be mediocre at best. And any program that is based upon mediocre program objectives will produce results and educational products that may be classified by the same name.

5. All behavioral objectives must be constantly evaluated and restated if they are to remain appropriate to meet the needs of the students. The standard of quality expected from this year's students may not be the same as that which will prevail tomorrow. *The goals for basic academic skills remain fairly stable.* The behavioral evaluation activities and criterion standards, however, are the parts of behavioral objectives that must be constantly changed to meet the needs of a particular group.

Chapter 2

BEHAVIORAL
OBJECTIVE
COMPONENTS

A large part of the discussions of disputants
comes from the want of accurate definition—
Let one define his terms and then stick to
the definition, and half the differences in
philosophy . . . would come to an end, and be
seen to have no real foundation.
—Tryon Edwards

OBJECTIVE

Students who have completed their study of this chapter should understand thoroughly the behavioral objective classifications and their component parts, so that when given a written test consisting of the following questions, 90 percent of the students will score at least 80 percent correct answers.

1. True–False (2 points each):
   (a) Performance objectives refer to all specific objectives that identify goals and strategy for evaluation. _____
   (b) All performance objectives can be classified as behavioral objectives. _____
   (c) The difference between a behavioral objective and a specific noninstructional objective consists of the differences in the minimum requirements for goal statements and evaluation criteria. _____
   (d) The primary concern in writing behavioral objectives is to improve communication. _____
   (e) The difference between a minimum level and desired level behavioral

objective is found in the addition of the criterion standard requirement for all desired level behavioral objectives. _____

(f) Procedural statements should always be included in desired level behavioral objectives. _____

(g) The use of the term "program objective" in place of the term "minimum level behavioral" is not appropriate since it implies too great a restriction upon the use of the minimum level behavioral objective. _____

(h) The future utilization of behavioral objectives in curriculum development probably depends upon teachers being able to write all behavioral objectives at the desired behavioral objective level. _____

(i) Goal statements attempt to identify the exact intended aim for which an objective is being written. _____

(j) One of the purposes of the three communication checks applied to the basic statement of each goal is to increase the confidence of the person writing the objectives in his own ability to write behavioral objectives. _____

2. Definitions (5 points each):
Define each of the following terms in short statements of 30 words or less.

   (a) Performance objective
   (b) Goal
   (c) Behavioral objectives
   (d) Minimum level behavioral objective
   (e) Desired level behavioral objective
   (f) Specific noninstructional objective

3. State the proper classification (minimum or desired level) for each of the following behavioral objectives (5 points each):

   (a) To improve the typewriting speed skills of all first-year typewriting students as measured by a five-minute timed writing at 30 net words per minute with no more than five errors by the end of the school year.

   (b) To improve fifth-grade pupils' skills in solving fractions as determined by a standardized fifth-grade arithmetic test in which the pupil answers correctly 84 out of 100 problems on fractions.

   (c) To improve the fourth-grade students' skills in map reading in social studies as determined by both oral and written teacher-made tests where 80% of the students will score 85% or above on the oral test and 75% of the students will score 75% or above on the written test.

   (d) To improve first-grade students' readiness in reading skills, as measured by a written teacher-made informal reading inventory.

   (e) To develop the ability of seventh-grade science students to identify and classify a mixed collection of rocks as determined by 90% of the students achieving an accuracy of 75% in placing the rocks in the three basic categories for classifying rocks.

   (f) To increase the speed of reading of eighth-grade students at Blount Middle School so that after a three-month period 85% of the students

show a 20% increase in words read per minute as measured
by SRA standardized speed-reading tests.

(g) For sixth-grade students to increase their ability to solve problems
involving rational numbers as determined by a written examination
prepared by the teacher.

(h) To improve the sixth-grade students' skills in solving fractions as
measured by a standardized sixth-grade arithmetic test on fractions.

(i) To improve Charlie Browns' serving skills in volleyball so that when
given one month to practice, he can take a serving skills accuracy test
and correctly serve over the net and within the proper boundary
lines 9 out of 10 attempts.

(j) To improve Snoopy's knowledge of circuit theory in electricity so
that given all of the necessary parts and materials, he can construct
and set up a three-way switch network.

(Answers follow bibliography at the end of the book.)

RELATIONSHIPS TO PERFORMANCE OBJECTIVES

In simple terms a *performance objective refers to any specifically stated
objective that identifies a goal and specifies some type of performance,
instrumentation, or other evaluation strategy that will furnish evidence
that the intended outcome of the goal has or has not been achieved.*
In Chapter 1 it was pointed out that both the instructional and noninstructional areas are subject to study and evaluation. It is clearly evi-
dent then that performance objectives must be stated to meet the needs
of both of these areas. The diagram shown in Figure 1 is designed to
illustrate possible uses and classifications of performance objectives.

PERFORMANCE OBJECTIVES	
Specific Noninstructional Objectives	Behavioral Objectives

1. Any nonlearner-oriented goal
   (a) structure or facility
   (b) educational processes
   (c) production of products such as materials, equipment, guide-lines, etc.
	1. Any learner-oriented goal designed to bring about a change in cognitive, affective, or psychomotor behavior
	   (a) teacher
	   (b) students
	   (c) others

Figure 1. Performance Objective Classifications

*Figure 1 reveals that both behavioral objectives and specific non-
instructional objectives are included within the broad definition of per-*

formance objectives. Thus, both types of performance objectives should consist of goal statements and evaluation. *The difference between a behavioral objective and a specific noninstructional objective consists of the difference in the minimum content requirements acceptable for the goal statements and evaluation criteria used in their development.* Each must communicate a reasonable message to its intended audience.

The emphasis of this text will be placed upon the behavioral objective category. However, Chapter 5 will introduce the writing of specific noninstructional objectives and furnish adequate examples. At this point it should be established that *the chief concern in writing performance objectives, particularly in the behavioral category, must be to improve communication between the writer and his intended audience.* Specifically speaking, the goal should be identified clearly and the evaluation criteria must be stated clearly and concisely.

The writing techniques recommended in this text are considered "a goals approach" to writing behavioral objectives. In past years, the goals of educational objectives (including some that have been stated in behavioral terms) have often been stated in terms of learnings that were either too vague or could not be measured adequately. In most instances concerning curriculum development, the initial decision of the teacher or program director will be to select and define the problem area in meaningful terms, with the scope and final delineation of the problem selected depending, at least in part, upon the specific objectives that are later identified in performance statements.

EXPLANATION AND DEFINITION OF
BEHAVIORAL OBJECTIVE COMPONENTS

Figure 2 illustrates the two levels of behavioral objectives referred to in this writing technique and shows the major components of each.

The information provided in Figure 2 reveals two levels of behavioral objectives and the two major parts of each, the goal and the evaluation activity. *These two parts may be completed separately and then joined together to make one complete objective.*

It is important to note that there is no reference to procedures in either of the two types of behavioral objectives shown. *The omission is intentional since procedures are not a part of a behavioral objective and should be separated from them.* Behavioral objectives identify goals and describe desired outcomes, whereas procedures usually describe the content, methods, treatments, strategies, processes, activities, or sequence of events that will take place in carrying out the design and evaluation activities. Teacher lesson plans may include the procedures.

BEHAVIORAL OBJECTIVES

I. MINIMUM LEVEL (Open-Ended)	II. DESIRED LEVEL (Closed-Ended)

A. Goal
  1. Basic statement
  2. Communication checks:
    (a) learner
    (b) program variable
    (c) implied behavioral domain
B. Evaluation
  E–1. Performance, activity, behavior, or instrumentation
    (a) optional statements
	A. Goal
	  1. Basic statement
	  2. Communication checks:
	    (a) learner
	    (b) program variable
	    (c) implied behavioral domain
	B. Evaluation
	  E–1. Performance, activity, behavior, or instrumentation
	    (a) optional statements
	  E–2. Expected success level or criterion
	    (a) optional statements

Figure 2. Behavioral Objective Components

Most studies provide a specific section in their format that is designed for the explanation of the procedures. Thus, there is little to be gained by trying to insert them again as part of a behavioral objective. In fact, much confusion may result by their use in the statement of objectives.

BEHAVIORAL OBJECTIVE

The term "behavioral objective" is used to identify a particular type of performance objective. It is interpreted as meaning a performance objective having an identifiable goal which identifies the learner, the program variable, and implies some type of learner behavioral change that can be evaluated as a direct outcome of the goal. This type of objective is a two component statement written in exact terms which includes the first component, the goal, and the second component, the outcome or evaluation of the goal. *Its key characteristic is that it not only states the goal but also identifies the instrumentation, performance, activity, or behavior the learner will become involved with as a means of evaluating the success he has achieved as an outcome of the intended goal of that particular objective.*

MINIMUM LEVEL BEHAVIORAL OBJECTIVE

The minimum level behavioral objective is the first step in a two-step classification of behavioral objectives arranged in hierarchial fashion. Objectives at this level give a complete basic statement of the goal and require that the goal statement meet the qualifications established by the three variables referred to as communication checks. In addition, the minimum level behavioral objective must state the performance, activity, instrumentation, or behavior that will be required of the learner in the evaluation of his achievement of the intended goal.

Some writers have referred to objectives of this type as "program objectives" because they do not include all of the specifics necessary for the desired level classification and because they are most frequently used to develop overall programs rather than to specify instructional classroom requirements. *There are many uses of the minimum level type of behavioral objective, and to refer to it as a "program objective" implies a restriction upon its use that is both erroneous and detrimental to the development of the behavioral objective movement.* Some of the reasons for writing behavioral objectives at the minimum level are as follows.

1. To denote exact program goals without specifying individual classroom specifics or evaluation criterions.
2. To prevent the evaluation activities and criterions from becoming too restrictive. This is particularly important in the higher level cognitive areas as well as in many affective domain areas.
3. To allow for individual differences based upon the idea that individual students should not be expected to react the same way in all situations or toward all common phenomena.
4. To prevent the error of placing too much emphasis upon measurement when there is substantial reason to question its appropriateness, validity, or reliability.
5. To encourage free-response creative type of evaluation activities in instances where no standards are available for the type of information that is desired.
6. To reduce the chances of requiring too much specificity, which in some instances may produce triviality rather than appropriate evaluation of the intended goal.
7. To increase teacher flexibility in both statement of goals and in planning of strategies for carrying out activities to obtain these goals.
8. To provide an alternative approach to behavioral objective develop-

ment when it is either impossible or impractical to develop an objective into the desired level classification.

Practically speaking, there are many goals in the behavioral sciences that do not lend themselves to the statement of a valid success level or single criterion that could be acceptable as "the" appropriate standard of performance for a particular objective. In such instances the behavioral objective should stop short of any attempt to force a "suspect" criterion into the behavioral objective statement just to be able to acknowledge that it has been written at a higher level.

In summing up this argument for minimum level behavioral objectives, we find that many times the use of an objective will not require the specifics furnished by the criterion or success level statement. Sometimes these objectives are prepared for system-wide use or for overall program guides for curriculum development activities or for individual projects. In these instances it is often better to let the individual teachers establish their own criterion standards based upon the students. The increased flexibility of this type of an objective would add substantially to meaningfulness of many objectives with a particular group of students. It is preferable to classify objectives by their level of development rather than to infer possible uses. *In fact, the entire future growth of the use of behavioral objectives in curriculum development and for instructional purposes may depend upon how well we can state and carry out objectives written at the minimum level.*

Goals

The term "goals" is used to identify the exact aim, purpose, or end that is to be obtained from any course of action or in any behavioral situation. The goal statement is the first part of any behavioral objective written by the technique presented in this text. Practically speaking, these goals are used as a point of departure from which the more specific and complete behavioral objective can be developed. An example might be:

> To increase the map-reading skills of
> sixth-grade students.

The example stated can be considered to be the basic statement of the goal. It is intended to identify the exact intended aim for which the objective is being written. The second step in writing the goal statement is to give it a communication check for three important variables. This means that upon careful examination the basic goal statement will be found to include (1) an identified program variable, (2) a distinct learner, and (3) an implied behavioral domain. The inclusion of an implied behavioral domain indicates that the objective is learner-oriented and will utilize some type of evaluation activity that will be sensitive to a change in student behavior.

The "how-to-do-it" uses of the three communication check variables will be explained in detail in Chapter 3, along with several examples of their use in completed goal statements. The purposes of the communication checks are: (1) to give the behavioral objective writer a method of checking his goal statements to see that they are complete, (2) to help ensure the audience, for which the objective is written, of receiving a reasonably clear communication of the intent of the objective, (3) to aid the writer in focusing more clearly upon what specific evaluation activity should be chosen for each objective, and (4) to improve the morale and confidence of the writer in his ability to produce quality behavioral objectives. The first three purposes are obvious, but the fourth should not be overlooked. The value of number four has been proved again and again in many workshops designed to train students and teachers to write behavioral objectives utilizing this goals-approach technique.

Briefly stated, the three communication check variables can be defined as follows...

1. Program variable: This component is the major concern of the writer and refers to the phenomenon that improves with a behavioral change in the learner. Normally the program variable in curriculum development or instructional research will be concerned with content area phenomena involving cognitive, affective, and psychomotor skills. It may, however, refer to organization, structure, facility, finance, process, and other variables, depending upon whether the objective is to become specific noninstructional or behavioral. The program variable can be determined in any of the performance objective classifications.

> Example: To increase the *map-reading skills*
> of sixth-grade students.

In this example "map-reading skills" is the program variable, phenomenon, or major behavioral concern of the teacher.

2. Learner: This refers to the identification of the person(s) who is (are) the primary recipient(s) of the benefits or behavioral changes offered by the objective. Usually this word will refer to some designated student or students, but it can also refer to staff members, lay

citizens, or any other person or group for which the objective has been written.

>Example: To increase the map-reading skills
>of *sixth-grade students.*

This example, which is the same one used to illustrate the program variable, clearly identifies "sixth-grade students" as the beneficiaries of the stated goal.

3. Implied behavioral domain: Bloom's (1956) use of the cognitive, affective, and psychomotor domains of behavior is the principal concern of this check on communication. These domains will be outlined more completely in Chapter 3. Our present concern is to explain the use of the term "implied." By referring to the examples used to illustrate program variable and learner, we find that in each instance there was a specific group of words in the goal statement that pinpointed each of these variables. "Map-reading skills" pinpointed the program variable, and "sixth-grade students" pinpointed the learners. Normally there is no specific group of words that are separated from the program variable to indicate the appropriate behavioral domain.

>Example: To increase the *map-reading skills*
>of *sixth-grade students.*

The behavioral objective writer in examining this goal statement would be able to determine that the primary concern of the objective would be to produce behavioral change in the cognitive area, since "skill in map-reading" would require a certain amount of recall information and might require both comprehension and application. In this instance he would diagnose the domain from the same group of three words that he had used in identifying the program variable.

Another reason that the behavioral domain is implied is that the program variable will not always clearly identify which of the three domains are the major concern. This identification may have to be traced back to the original need, or can be determined by observation of the evaluation data that is to be collected. For purposes of our present discussion, we will assume the goal is being written and no evaluation activities have yet been selected.

>Example: To improve the *teamwork* in playing
>basketball of the *seventh-grade students.*

Here we find that teamwork or teamwork in playing basketball is the program variable and that seventh-grade students are the learners. We cannot determine completely from this statement which of the three domains is intended. In fact, all three may be included in the intent of the goal statement. If the coach sees the need as being lack of information, he would place it in the cognitive domain. If, however, the original need appeared to be attitude or poor ball control, he might very appropriately classify the domain as either affective or psychomotor.

Another example might be the use of a program variable such as handwriting skill. Most teachers would classify this as a psychomotor activity. However, if students have never received instruction on how to hold a pencil or how to make certain writing movements, it could become cognitive-oriented or perhaps both cognitive and psychomotor.

The major concern of the behavioral objective writer is to be sure that some behavioral domain is indicated in the goal. If this is not done the objective will end up being specific noninstructional. The implied behavioral domain presents no problem to the writer of an objective since he knows the original need upon which the objective is based and can design the goal statement to suit his own diagnosis. The implied domain check is to help the writer be more certain that (1) he has selected the appropriate program variable, (2) the objective is behavioral and not specific noninstructional, and (3) he can choose the appropriate evaluation activities.

Evaluation

Evaluation of goal achievement in behavioral objectives has all of the problems inherent to evaluation in the behavioral sciences. The two primary concerns are (1) what behavioral observations can be used as valid indications of change and (2) how to establish standards by which to judge performance. The nature of the minimum level behavioral objective and the reasons for its utilization require that we address ourselves only to the first concern stated. That is, if the objective is to meet the minimum qualification necessary for it to be referred to as a behavioral objective, it must identify some behavior or instrumentation that the learner will perform that will supply data for evaluation of the achievement of the intended goal.

Chapter 4 refers to this evaluation component as being the E-1 (evaluation-first part) and gives several examples of how such evaluations may be stated. As illustrated in Figure 2, a key part of the E-1 component may be the optional statements that are included to ensure better communication of the objective to its intended audience. These optional statements provide information on any special considerations that are thought to be necessary to fully explain the intent of the evaluation component.

> Example: To train students in vocational electronics
> to understand the function and be able to make
> use of all component parts of a television set
> so that, *given all of the correct parts necessary,*
> *including a schematic diagram and tools, each*
> *can construct a television set.*

In this example the E-1 evaluation component began with the word "given" and included the remainder of the objective statement. The E-1 activity was to construct a television set, and all of the information provided from the word "given" through the word "tools" can be considered as optional information provided to better communicate the evaluation process.

DESIRED LEVEL BEHAVIORAL OBJECTIVE

The desired level behavioral objective can be considered as being the second step in the two-step classification of behavioral objectives, or the top of the hierarchical classification of performance objectives. *Objectives written at this level include the two major components, goals and evaluation, stated for the minimum level behavioral objectives. In addition to the goal and evaluation components already stated, the desired level objective requires a criterion standard as to the expected success level that the learner should obtain in his evaluation activity.*

This type of behavioral objective has frequently been referred to by other writers as a classroom or instructional objective. This is because it is a closed-loop type of objective that has all of the necessary specifics included to make it functional for classroom use. As was the case with the minimum level behavioral objective, the term "classroom" or "instructional objective" is too restrictive to give an accurate description of its value. In addition to classroom use, it can be substituted for any minimum level objective, is advocated for use with research projects, and is preferred in the development of proposals for funded projects.

Theoretically, all behavioral objectives would be written in the desired level category if appropriate behavioral observations and criterion standards were available for purposes of evaluation. Since this is not the case, it is probably better to distinguish between the two classifications of objectives by referring to the type rather than to their use.

The writing of the desired level behavioral objective requires additional knowledge and expertise over and above that required by the other two levels. The development of this type of objective demands both technical competence in the mechanics of writing behavioral objectives and a substantial amount of subject-matter competence. For this reason, objectives of this nature are often written by teaching teams that have subject-area competency in common.

The basic goal statement, communication checks, and E-1 evaluation component are the same for the desired level objective as for the minimum level objective. In addition, the desired level objective includes a statement of the criterion standards or success level expected from the learner. Chapter 4 refers to the success level as the E-2 (evaluation-second part) and cites several examples of objectives written in this classification. This E-2 component, which in public school classroom teacher use usually states the teacher expectancy and learner requirement, is what elevates this type of behavioral objective from the minimum level to the desired level. As was the case with the E-1 component, the E-2 component may also include optional statements that help identify more clearly the intent of the evaluation component.

> Example: To train students in vocational electronics
> to understand the function and be able to
> make use of all component parts of a
> television set so that, given all the correct
> parts necessary, including a schematic
> diagram and tools, each can construct
> a television set *and have it operating*
> *efficiently according to the subjective*
> *judgment of the instructor in less than*
> *eight (8) class periods.*

This example, which is an extension of the same example used to illustrate the minimum level behavioral objective, includes an E-2 statement from the word "and" (following the words "television set") to the end of the objective. The E-1 statement indicated the learner would have to construct a television set. The E-2 statement established that the standard by which the constructed television set would be judged or the success level required of the students would be for the set to operate efficiently according to the subjective judgment of the instructor. The operational success had not been specified in the minimum level statement. In addition, the E-2 component included one optional statement specifying that the entire evaluation procedure would have to be completed within eight class periods. This optional statement could just as well have been included as part of the "given" along with the reference to parts, diagram, and tools. In any event the teacher made a value judgment as to the appropriate amount of time that should be allowed and specified the eight class periods as meaningful requirement in light of the way he viewed the assignment.

This example did not include the use of the teacher expectancy criterion. It could be included by changing the E-2 component to read as follows: ". . . and eighty-five percent (85%) of the students will have it operating efficiently, according to the subjective judgment of the instructor, in less than eight (8) class periods." The teacher expectancy allows the instructor to state his expectancy more realistically or to obtain his own goal without expecting perfection on the part of the students. Chapter 4 will handle the entire evaluation strategy in much greater detail. The present explanation should sufficiently explain the information in Figure 2.

Note: Chapters 3, 4, and 5 of this book are considered to be the writing-technique teaching chapters. In these chapters many examples are used to aid the development of writing and critiquing skills. The reader may be interested in knowing in advance that none of the examples is artificial, but represent the first efforts of teachers to write behavioral objectives for their own classroom program after having attended one behavioral objective workshop using this goal approach technique. Additional information on these initial writing efforts follows the last behavioral objective example stated in Chapter 5, prior to the discussion of specific noninstructional objectives.

Chapter 3

DEVELOPING GOAL STATEMENTS

The secret of success is *constancy to purpose.*
   —Disraeli

There is no road to success but through a
clear, strong purpose.
   —T. T. Munger

The man without a purpose is like a ship
without a rudder.
   —Carlyle

OBJECTIVE
The objective of this chapter is for the reader to be able to apply his knowledge of how to develop goal statements by the communication check technique, so that given the following five goal statements he can critique in writing each of the five goals correctly without error in the general classification of the three communication check variables.

1. For elementary school children to develop skill in performing rhythmic movement to music.

2. For sixth-grade science students to develop skill in classifying selected objects.

3. To improve the reading comprehension skills of third-grade students.

4. To develop in first-grade students the ability to illustrate one-to-one correspondence, determine the number cardinality of the set, order sets, and manipulate sets to demonstrate basic operations.

    5. To increase college students' appreciation for the use
of behavioral objectives in curriculum development.

(Answers follow bibliography at the end of the book.)

THE BASIC STATEMENT

Formulating the basic statement of a goal is relatively easy and requires
very little expertise for teachers or program planners to fulfill the minimum requirements for its acceptance. The teacher or program planner
thinks back to the original need that was the basis for writing the objective in the first place, and then decides what change he would like to
see occur that holds promise for improving the situation. With reference
to selection of the basic statement of the goal, there is no difference
between the two behavioral objective classifications as shown in Figure
2 (p. 17). In each instance the goal statement primarily represents the
identification of an exact aim, intent, or purpose that is to be obtained
from a specific course of action. Some examples of basic goal statements are:

1. To increase the rate and level of achievement and skill in the use of
   scientific processes by third-grade students.
2. To increase the achievement in word study skills of second-grade
   students.
3. To increase Johnny Smith's speed and improve his endurance.
4. To improve the fundamental locomotor and axile movements of
   grade-one students.
5. For fifth-grade students to develop the ability to identify and relate
   precautions to basic health hazards that exist in school, home, and
   community.
6. For fourth-grade students to learn to interpret symbols on maps
   and globes.
7. For sixth-grade children to develop the ability to sight-read music.
8. To improve antisocial eleventh-grade students' attitudes toward
   classmates and teachers.
9. To improve the ability of tenth-grade general mathematics students
   to solve decimal fractions involving tenths, hundredths, and thousandths.
10. For workshop participants to become proficient in the technical
    skills necessary to write good behavioral objectives.

THE COMMUNICATION CHECK

Each statement of a goal in a behavioral objective should include three
components: (1) an implied behavioral domain, (2) the learner(s) involved, and (3) the program variable. These components may be defined
as follows:

Behavioral domain

This refers to Bloom's (1956) use of the cognitive, affective, and psychomotor domains of behavior.

1. *Cognitive domain:* All behaviors dealing with the recall or recognition of knowledge and the development of intellectual abilities and
   skills. The taxonomy divides the cognitive domain into six areas.
2. *Affective domain:* All behaviors that describe changes in interest,
   attitudes, and values, and the development of appreciations and adequate adjustment.
3. *Psychomotor domain:* All behaviors that are primarily concerned
   with the performance of a physical activity.

It is not necessary to utilize the educational objective taxonomies
in order for program planners to *learn* the mechanics for writing behavioral objectives. Trying to use the taxonomies as the primary basis
for learning the techniques may become self-defeating. In many instances the time and effort required for teachers to remember all of the
various knowledge levels and definitions as stated in the taxonomy will
lead to considerable frustration in the development of skill in writing
behavioral objectives. The educational taxonomies have their value in
training educators to write objectives at different learning levels or levels
of understanding, but mastery of the taxonomies should not become
a part of the instruction required in learning the writing techniques. The
important point in checking the basic goal statements for communication is that the teacher needs to be able to recognize whether or not
the statement implies or infers one or more of the three domains; this
information can then be used as both a check in analyzing the type of
objective they have communicated to the reader and in the selection of
the evaluation activity.

Learner

This component refers to the identification of the person(s) who is (are)
expected to have a change in behavior or who is (are) the primary
recipient(s) of the benefits offered by the objective. Usually this will refer

to students, staff members, lay persons from the community, or any learner.

Program variable

Normally the program variable in curriculum and instructional research will be concerned with organization, content area, or skill. However, it may refer to structure (facility), finance in some instances, and to other variables depending upon whether the objective is to become specific noninstructional or behavioral.

Examples of how these communication checks may be applied to the basic statements of goals previously listed may be seen by restating the goals and using the numbers 1, 2, 3, 4, and 5 to indicate which words are used to identify the various elements of every stated goal. In each instance (1) refers to cognitive domain, (2) affective domain, (3) psychomotor domain, (4) learner, and (5) the program variable. The following examples illustrate how goals may be given communication checks.

1. To increase the rate and level of achievement (1) and skill (1) in the use of scientific processes (1,5) of third-grade students (4).
   Critique:
   (a) Learner—third-grade students.
   (b) Program variable—scientific processes.
   (c) Behavioral domain—cognitive (achievement and skill in the use of scientific processes seems to imply primarily the use of cognitive understandings).
   (d) Communicates—goal communicates at least at the minimum level of communication since all of the checks are accounted for.
2. To increase the achievement (1) in word (1,5) study (1,5) skills (1,5) of second-grade students (4).
   Critique:
   (a) Learner—second-grade students.
   (b) Program variable—word study skills.
   (c) Behavioral domain—cognitive (achievement in word study skills implies cognitive behavior).
   (d) Communicates—all checks accounted for.
3. To increase Johnny Smith's (4) speed (3,5) and improve his endurance (3,5) in running (3,5) one mile (5).

Critique:
  (a) Learner—Johnny Smith.
  (b) Program variable—speed and endurance in running one mile.
  (c) Behavioral domain—psychomotor (speed and enudrance in running implies primarily physical activity).
  (d) Communicates—all checks accounted for.

4. To improve the fundamental locomotor (3,5) and axile (3,5) movements (3,5) of grade-one students (4).
  Critique:
  (a) Learner—grade-one students.
  (b) Program variable—fundamental locomotor and axile movements.
  (c) Behavioral domain—psychomotor (locomotor and axile movements imply physical activity).
  (d) Communicates—all checks accounted for.

5. For fifth-grade students (4) to develop the ability (1,5) to identify (1,5) and relate (1,5) precautions (1,5) to basic health hazards (1,5) that exist in school (1,5), home (1,5), and community (1,5).
  Critique:
  (a) Learner—fifth-grade students.
  (b) Program variable—ability to identify and relate precautions to basic health hazards that exist in school, home, and community.
  (c) Behavioral domain—cognitive (developing the ability in the above-stated program variable implies cognitive behavior).
  (d) Communicates—all checks accounted for.

6. For fourth-grade students (4) to learn to interpret (1) symbols (1,5) on maps (5) and globes (5).
  Critique:
  (a) Learner—fourth-grade students.
  (b) Program variable—symbols on maps ad globes.
  (c) Behavioral domain—cognitive (learning to interpret symbols implies cognitive behavior).
  (d) Communicates—all checks accounted for.

7. For sixth-grade children 4) to improve their ability (1) to sight-read (1,5) music (5).

Critique:
(a) Learner—sixth-grade children.
(b) Program variable—sight-read music.
(c) Behavioral domain—cognitive (ability to sight-read implies cognitive behavior).
(d) Communicates—all checks accounted for.

8. To improve antisocial eleventh-grade students' (4) attitudes (2,5) toward (5) classmates (5) and teachers (5).
Critique:
(a) Learner—antisocial eleventh-grade students.
(b) Program variable—attitudes toward classmates and teachers.
(c) Behavioral domain—affective (attitudes imply affective behavior).
(d) Communicates—all checks accounted for.

9. To improve the ability of tenth-grade general mathematics students (4) to solve (1) decimal (1,5) fractions (1,5) involving tenths (5), hundredths (5), and thousandths (5).
Critique:
(a) Learner—tenth-grade general mathematics students.
(b) Program variable—decimal fractions involving tenths, hundredths, and thousandths.
(c) Behavioral domain—cognitive (solving decimal fractions implies cognitive behavior).
(d) Communicates—all checks accounted for.

10. For workshop participants (4) to become proficient in the technical skills (5) necessary to write (1,5) good behavioral objectives (1,5).
Critique:
(a) Learner—workshop participants.
(b) Program variable—technical skills necessary to write good behavioral objectives.
(c) Behavioral domain—cognitive (writing good behavioral objectives implies cognitive behavior).
(d) Communicates—all checks accounted for.

Note that the program variable and the behavioral domain can be identified in some goal statements by reference to just one or two words. At other times it may seem more appropriate to select key words and all of their modifiers. Since the critique process is designed primarily as a self-checking exercise for the behavioral objective writer's own benefit, it does not make any difference which approach he uses: Either single words or groups of words will accomplish the same purpose. Sometimes the program variable will be found in two or more parts of the objective and the parts may be separated from each other. Again, this makes no difference. The important consideration is that all of the variables must be identifiable and stated in a reasonable fashion.

All of the example goal statements listed here were written by classroom teachers attending behavioral objective workshops. No value judgments have been made concerning their appropriateness for prescribed teacher area of interest. They are used solely for the purpose of illustrating how goal statements can be critiqued or checked for communication. Any goal component of a behavioral objective that identifies each of the three communication components—implied behavioral domain, learner, and program variable—will assure the writer that he has communicated his intent or purpose to the audience at least reasonably well.

It is obvious from these examples that goal statements in the behavioral objective category will have a direct relationship between the words used to identify the program variable and the implied behavioral domain. The reason the behavioral domain is always referred to as being *implied* is that in many instances no one but the writer of the objective can really know from the goal statement standing alone whether the intended behavior will be cognitive, affective, or psychomotor. Variables such as teamwork could be any one or all of the three behaviors. Handwriting skill can be cognitive or psychomotor. Only the writer of the objective knows the original need upon which the objective is based. The reader can, however, tell more certainly what the behavioral domain is intended to be after the evaluation activities are attached to the goal statement.

Now let us examine another goal statement that was taken directly from a funded project concerned with communication skill development.

To establish reading laboratories in all secondary schools.
Critique:
(a) Learner—none stated.
(b) Program variable—reading laboratories.
(c) Behavioral domain—no behavioral domain implied
(d) Communicates—does not communicate as a goal that would be acceptable in a behavioral objective.

This example illustrates the need for the communication checks as well as for the specific noninstructional objective writing technique discussed in Chapter 5. Any time there is no behavioral domain implied in the goal statement, the objective is either poorly stated or is not intended to be placed into the behavioral objectives classification. It still can become a good performance objective provided appropriate evaluation activities are later spelled out for evaluating the outcomes of the intended goal.

Additional teacher-prepared sample goal statements to critique for communication checks:

1. To develop in Head Start children counting skills utilizing numbers 1 through 10.
2. To extend the science achievement of second-grade children.
3. To improve the performance of balance beam skills of junior high school girls.
4. To increase the basketball skill level of tenth-grade boys.
5. To increase the map-reading skills of seventh-grade children in social studies classes.
6. To extend the achievement and skill of county personnel in writing behavioral objectives.
7. To improve reading comprehension skills of third-grade reading students.
8. To improve the fine motor skills of paper cutting and crayon work of kindergarten students.
9. To increase seventh-grade pupils' achievement in social studies basic skills.
10. To improve the achievement and skills in speaking and writing of fifth-grade students.
11. To improve the skill of fifth-grade library aides in carding books.
12. To improve the interest and attitudes of fifth-grade students in library skills.
13. To improve the comprehension of fifth-grade students in the use of the Dewey Decimal System.
14. To develop in teachers the ability to write behavioral objectives.
15. To increase the interest of fifth-grade students in bird watching.
16. To improve the performance of batting skills of fifth-grade boys.
17. To improve the skills of elementary principals in Polk County in writing behavioral objectives.
18. To improve the rope-jumping skills of fifth-grade students.

19. To provide opportunity in a physical education program in grades K–12 for boys and girls to develop coordination and motor skills adaptable to their age and grade level.
20. To improve the skills and achievement in the use of the globe in social studies.
21. To improve the skill of recognizing new vocabulary words in a second-grade reading class.
22. To improve the blocking and tackling skills of high school football players.
23. To develop word recognition skills of fourth-grade reading students.
24. To develop in all teachers of Manatee County schools an appreciation for writing behavioral objectives.
25. To improve the sewing skills of ninth-grade home economics students.
26. To increase the reading achievement levels of children placed in learning disability classes.
27. To increase the first-grade students' awareness of colors and vowel sounds in the words in color-reading program.
28. To improve softball skills of second-grade girls.
29. To improve the achievement and skills in typing of high school students.
30. To increase the physical skills and coordination necessary in primary school children to play rhythm band instruments.
31. For all ninth-grade algebra students to attain the ability to solve a quadratic equation.
32. To improve the achievement of dividing fractions of sixth-grade children.
33. To develop the ability of the tenth-grade home economics students to write balanced menus.
34. To increase the skill in multiplying three-digit numbers by two-digit numbers of fourth-grade students.
35. To improve sight-reading of music in sixth-grade pupils.
36. To instill an awareness and acquisition of vocabulary development and skills in third-grade reading students.
37. To improve fifth-grade pupils' computational skills in addition of whole numbers.
38. To develop an appreciation of poetry in fourth-grade children.
39. To increase eighth-grade pupils' achievement in mathematics skills.

40. To develop an enthusiastic interest in learning good study habits among junior high students.
41. To improve ability for solving written problems in the eleventh-grade algebra course.
42. To increase the skill of seventh-grade students in computing the sums of rational numbers.
43. To increase the mathematics knowledge of eighth-grade students in the basic math classes.
44. To improve county personnel's attitude toward writing behavior objectives.
45. To develop an understanding of the Constitution by high school students in American history classes.
46. To help make tenth- and eleventh-grade students aware of the "dignity of labor."
47. To improve the attitude of transferred junior high pupils toward their new school community.
48. To develop in a twelfth-grade music composition class the ability to compose in classical style a string quartet of 64 measures in length, showing awareness of tones, qualities, and practical pitch range of the instruments being written for.
49. To improve the ability of kindergarten students to recognize the correct names of various animals.
50. To increase the skills of proper selection and usage of tools of students in a beginning small engines class.

Chapter 4

IDENTIFICATION OF EVALUATION ACTIVITIES

When God made Heaven and God made Earth,
He formed the seas and gave Man birth.
His heart was full of jubilation;
But he made one error—no Evaluation!

Oh, He said, "That's good!" and He meant it, too.
But now we know that that won't do.
Even something that we know is best,
We've got to prove by a pre-post test.
  —NASA Newsletter

OBJECTIVE

The objective of this chapter is for students to be able to comprehend and apply their knowledge of how to write behavioral objective evaluation statements utilizing the E–1 and E–2 component techniques so that given the following 10 evaluation statements, 90 percent of the students will score 80 percent or higher on a written critique involving all 10 statements.

Note: Critique each of the evaluation components in the following behavioral objectives by underscoring the E-1's, placing parentheses around the E-2's, and writing the classification (minimum or desired level) at the end of such evaluation statement.

1. To develop in ninth-grade agriculture students a basic knowledge of function, composition, and properties of soil to be measured by a written teacher-made test on which 70% of the students correctly respond to 15 out of 28 questions.

2. To develop the understanding ability of all foreign language students as determined by students being able to follow and translate words in a paragraph prepared by the classroom teacher.

3. To develop in students an understanding of the values which affect individual behavior and family living as measured by a written teacher-made test in which 80% of students are able to list 70% of the values previously presented in class.

4. To develop a better understanding of the fundamental skills in the use of tools and materials of seventh-graders as measured by pupils using various tools or materials selected by the teacher for evaluation purposes.

5. To increase the tenth-grade language arts students ability to recall the information given by panels and in group discussions as measured by a written teacher-made test on which students can identify those major ideas covered by the panel or in the group discussion.

6. To improve the ability of seventh-grade students to compute rationale numbers as measured by a written teacher-made test, so that at least 51% of the students can correctly work 25 out of 35 problems.

7. To develop the ability of seventh-grade students to measure lengths in metric system and other standards as measured by a written teacher-made test in which 75% of the students measure correctly 8 out of 10 objects using two different standards for each object.

8. To have eighth-grade American History students recognize how the Industrial Revolution in England affected America as determined by a teacher-made written test on which the student can identify the appropriate changes in American society with 51% of the students scoring 70% or better.

9. To develop an understanding among seventh-grade social studies students that the most important differences in human behavior are learned, not inherited as measured by a written teacher-made test on which 75% of the students tested score correctly 8 out of 10 questions.

10. To develop in eighth-grade students the ability to graph solution sets of open sentences as measured by a 10-item teacher-made test so that 51% of the students score 70% or better.

(Answers follow bibliography at the end of the book.)

EVALUATION

Evaluation, as used in this book, refers to the performance, activity, behavior, or instrumentation that will be utilized as a means of demonstrating the level of success achieved as an outcome of the goal statement in each particular objective. These evaluation activities may be verbal, nonverbal, manipulative, or any other type of performance, provided it is appropriate for measuring the goal as stated in the behavioral objective. The evaluation activities may be stated in one short sentence or may include several sentences when appropriate.

The primary concerns of evaluation are to (1) select the most meaningful type of evaluation activity, (2) establish standards as criterion measures of success, and (3) determine how to collect the desired data without contaminating the results. Each of these concerns becomes increasingly difficult to accomplish as we approach the higher levels of cognitive or psychomotor behaviors, and the proper determination of standards and data collection methods is virtually nonexistent in many of the affective domain classifications. We must observe what the learner does in the form of overt behavior, or what he says he feels or thinks.

Normal conditions for learner observation for overt behavior are seldom available. Thus, we must secure information most of the time from student talk, personal involvement, writing, or close association with the variable under consideration. And even with these methods we must be careful, in the affective domain areas, not to let the learner know what response is desired, or he may supply it for that reason alone.

Most evaluation of objectives will take the form of tests that attempt to determine how successful the students and/or teachers have been in achieving the objective's intended goal. These tests may be standardized or specially constructed by the teacher or staff. In some instances, however, no objective measurement may be available and evaluation must be carried out by subjective measures, such as clinical observation or teacher judgment. In either event it must be kept in mind that the evaluation processes utilized are means to an end and have no intrinsic values of their own. In other words tests are used for the sake of evaluation of objectives, and not the other way around. The evaluation of objectives will in some instances merely involve observation of physical motor movement activities. In fact, evaluation can involve the observation or measurement of any activity that can show a change in a phenomenon that is specified by the goal statement.

Objectives can be stated for either short-term or long-range results. They can be concerned with either individual skills or large units of instruction. In either case the statement of evaluation should reflect the type of data that will be appropriate for evaluation of the specific goal of each objective. For evaluating some instructional projects, it may be necessary to use control groups along with the experimental ones to establish comparisons between the participants. If standardized tests are used, they may best be employed in long-range longitudinal or cross-sectional time studies. In this event, system norms may serve as better indicators of progress and comparisons than will the national norms.

There are both advantages and disadvantages to the utilization of normed tests. The type of information desired by the teacher or decisionmaker will determine how this data is utilized. It should be pointed out, however, that with the present emphasis upon the individualization of the student, including individualization through individualized statements of behavioral objectives, comparisons of students against each other should be minimized.

The idea of *individualization* of students through behavioral objective writing is necessitated since students not only have many similar characteristics but also many differences. If we really mean what we so often verbalize concerning meeting the needs of children, we must to some extent plan for and measure the degree to which a school program is successful in the discovery and development of individual abilities, interests, and talents. It is obvious that education based upon individual differences will, at least in part, require statements of behavioral objectives that are unique to the person or persons involved. Often this measure of school quality will be difficult, and sometimes it will require the development of special evaluation devices that measure the particular performance expected from each child as a result of the adopted program.

Instrumentation or performance (E-1)

The basic statement of evaluation that will be joined onto the goal statement in writing performance objectives was referred to in Figure 2 (p. 17), as the E-1 (evaluation-first part) or the naming of the performance, activity, behavior, or instrumentation that will be necessary in order to evaluate the outcome of each particular goal. The identification of the E-1 requires that the teacher or program planner know his subject area or content material well enough to be able to determine the appropriateness of the evaluative measure he intends to use. In many instances this will require that the teacher or project director call in consultant help to aid in selecting meaningful instruments. Whoever is in charge of the evaluation processes will need to be concerned with (1) context in which the program will operate, (2) processes or activities to be employed in the program, (3) type and sources of information to be collected, (4) how the data will be organized and analyzed, and (5) how the data will be reported.

Repeating from our previous definition, we observe that a key characteristic of evaluation is that it must state what behavior, performance, or activity the learner will be doing when he has achieved the goal of that particular objective. In many instances this may be accomplished by simply identifying the instrumentation that will be utilized, such as a written or standardized test. This then becomes the chief criterion upon which the basic statement of evaluation is based. A check for the adequacy of the basic evaluation statement may be made by determining in advance whether or not the activity will furnish acceptable evidence that the objective has or has not been achieved.

An example of the basic statement (E-1) can be seen in the following:

> To train workshop participants in the mechanical
> skills required for writing behavioral objectives *as
> evaluated by a written examination.*

In this example the goal statement of the objective includes the entire sentence through the word "objectives," and the E-1 or instrumentation of evaluation is shown in italics. According to our previous definitions of performance objectives, this example would represent a minimum level behavioral objective since it includes a statement of the goal that can be checked by the three communication check factors and in addition, identifies the instrumentation to be utilized or if the behavioral objective writer prefers to refer to a behavioral activity, this can be seen as involving writing on the part of the workshop participants.

Figure 2 refers to optional statements that may be included in either the E-1 or E-2 components of evaluation. These optional statements are included at the discretion of the writer. The purpose of the optional statements is to ensure the best possible communication between the writer and the intended audience. Optional statements usually include pertinent givens and/or conditions that are deemed necessary to fully explain the intent of the evaluation process. Any special considerations that are thought to be necessary for better communication can be stated as part of the optional statements.

The use of optional statements can be illustrated by altering the previous example of a minimum level behavioral objective.

> To train workshop participants in the mechanical
> skills required for writing behavioral objectives,
> as evaluated by a written examination *including*

> *questions requiring the writing of behavioral
> objectives* and a *one-hour time limit for completion
> of the test.*

This objective now includes in the E-1 portion two optional statements (in italics) that were not part of the previous example.

Expected success level (E-2)

The E-2 (evaluation-second part) component refers to certain criteria for writing evaluation statements. These criteria will better ensure that the standard or criterion measure in the completed behavioral objective has sufficient merit to make the objective meaningful. It is this E-2 component stating the success level expected of the learner (and sometimes the teacher expectancy) that elevates this type of a behavioral objective from the minimum level to the desired level behavioral. In other words, the activity is not only identified as in E-1, but how well the learner is expected to perform the activity is also clearly defined, along with the teacher's expectancy when this criterion is applicable. Using our previous examples, we now can relate the E-2 statement to the completed behavioral objective by rewording the E-1 and adding the success level expected.

> To train workshop participants in the mechanical
> skills required for writing behavioral objectives,
> as evaluated by a one-hour written examination,
> including questions requiring the writing of
> behavioral objectives, *on which 90% of the work-
> shop participants will obtain at least
> 8 correct answers for the 10 questions given
> on the examination.*

Reworded, we might have stated the E-2 to read: ". . . on which 90% of the workshop participants will obtain 80% correct answers." In this example the reference to 90% of the workshop participants refers to the hoped-for success or expectancy of the instructor, whereas 80% correct answers refers to the level of success expected from the students. The E-2 component of the evaluation statement may utilize various types of criteria for indicating the level of expected success. The number of correct responses and percentage statements are probably used most frequently. However, it is possible to utilize time limits (such as in measurements of track performances), grade placement, and any other criterion that best represents the standard to be obtained.

To analyze the behavioral objective written at the desired level, we might break it down into the following component parts.

A. Goal
   1. Basic statement—To train workshop participants in the mechanical skills required for writing behavioral objectives.
   2. Communication checks
     (a) Learner—workshop participants.
     (b) Program variable—mechanical skills . . . for writing behavioral objectives.
     (c) Implied domain—cognitive (implied from "skills . . . for writing behavioral objectives").
B. Evaluation
   1. E-1 (performance or instrumentation)—". . . as evaluated by a written examination."
     (a) Optional statements—"one hour" and "including questions requiring the writing of behavioral objectives."
   2. E-2 (expected success level—". . . on which 90% of the workshop participants will obtain at least 8 correct answers for the 10 questions given on the examination."
     (a) Optional statements—none.
     (b) In this E-2 statement the "90% of the workshop participants" represents teacher expectancy, and "8 correct answers for the 10 questions given" refers to student requirement.

SAMPLE EVALUATION STATEMENTS

In Chapter 3 there were 10 goal statements given as examples for goal statement critique purposes. We will restate these goals and specify some sample evaluation activities that could be used in the development of the sample goal statements into performance objectives.

   1. *Goal:*
To increase the rate and level of achievement and skill in the use of scientific processes of third-grade students.
Evaluation:
As determined by appropriate standardized tests, special competency tests, and teacher appraisal.

Critique:
(a) E-1—instrumentation or evaluation activities stated by reference to tests and appraisal.
(b) E-2—none.
(c) Optional statements—none.
(d) Classification—minimum level behavioral.

2. *Goal:*
To increase the learning achievement in word study skills of second-grade students.
Evaluation:
As measured by the Primary I Battery of the Stanford Achievement Test for Word Study Skills on which 90% of the students score at grade level or above.
Critique:
(a) E-1—instrumentation identified by the test reference.
(b) E-2—"90% of the students" represents teacher expectancy, and "score at grade level or above" is student requirement.
(c) Optional statements—none.
(d) Classification—desired level behavioral.

3. *Goal:*
To increase Johnny Smith's speed and improve his endurance.
Evaluation:
So that given a stopwatch and an official measured 440-yard track, he will run one mile in less time than his best previous effort of 5 minutes and 32 seconds.
Critique:
(a) E-1—"he will run one mile" is the evaluation performance or behavior.
(b) E-2—"in less time than his best previous effort of 5 minutes and 32 seconds" represents success level or student requirement.
(c) Optional statements—"so that given a stopwatch and an official measured 440-yard track" is optional statement for E-1.
(d) Classification—desired level behavioral.

4. *Goal:*
To improve the fundamental locomotor and axile movements of grade-one students.

Evaluation:
So that 80% of the students can perform correctly 75% of all the locomotor and axile movements described in a teacher-made test.

Critique:
(a) E-1—performing locomotor and axile movements from a teacher-made test describes behaviors and type of instrumentation.
(b) E-2—"80% of the students" refers to teacher expectancy and "performing correctly 75% of the movements" is student requirement.
(c) Optional statements—none.
(d) Classification—desired level behavioral.

5. *Goal:*
For fifth-grade students to develop the ability to identify and relate precautions to basic health hazards that exist in school, home, and community.

Evaluation:
As measured by a teacher-made test of 10 questions in which 80% of the students will answer correctly 8 of the 10 questions.

Critique:
(a) E-1—teacher-made test of 10 questions is instrumentation.
(b) E-2—"80% of the students" is teacher expectancy, whereas "answer correctly 8 of the 10 questions" is student requirement.
(c) Optional statements—none.
(d) Classification—desired level behavioral.

6. *Goal:*
For fourth-grade students to learn to interpret symbols on maps and globes.

Evaluation:
So that when given a specific geographical location and an appropriate map and globe, 80% of the students can perform the interpretation of the symbols in the given area of each with 75% accuracy, according to the teacher's observation and judgment.

Critique:
(a) E-1—performance, activity, or behavior is to interpret symbols on a map or globe.
(b) E-2—"80% of the students" is the teacher expectancy and "75% accuracy" is the student requirement.

      (c) Optional statements—E-2 optional statement is "so that when given a specific geographical location and an appropriate map and globe."

      (d) Classification—desired level behavioral.

7. *Goal:*

For sixth-grade children to improve their ability to sight-read music.

Evaluation:

So that when given two weeks instruction on the flutophone, 75% of the children can either sight-read without error a form measure exercise devised by the teacher that includes only those notes taught during the instructional program or improve their preassessment test scores by 10%.

Critique:

      (a) E-1—behavioral activities are to sight-read without error a form measure exercise devised by the teacher and to take a preassessment test.

      (b) E-2—"75% of the children" is teacher expectancy, without error and 10% improvement in test scores are alternative student requirements.

      (c) Optional statements—E-1 option is "that includes only those notes taught during the instructional program." E-2 option is "so that given two weeks instruction on the flutophone." This last option could be considered for both E-1 and E-2.

      (d) Classification—desired level behavioral.

8. *Goal:*

To improve antisocial eleventh-grade students' attitudes toward classmates and teachers.

Evaluation:

As determined by scores obtained on sociometric tests, teacher ratings, and student-teacher attitude surveys.

Critique:

      (a) E-1—the tests, ratings, and surveys represent instrumentation.

      (b) E-2—none.

      (c) Optional statements—none.

      (d) Classification—minimum level behavioral.

9. *Goal:*

To improve the ability of tenth-grade general mathematics

students to solve decimal fractions involving tenths, hundredths, and thousandths.

Evaluation:

As measured by a teacher-constructed test of 100 problems on which 90% of the students answer 75% of the problems correctly.

Critique:

(a) E-1—a teacher-constructed test of 100 problems identifies instrumentation.

(b) E-2—"90% of the students" is teacher expectancy. "Answer 75% of the problems correctly" is student requirement.

(c) Optional statements—none.

(d) Classification—desired level behavioral.

10. *Goal:*

For workshop participants to become proficient in the technical skills necessary to write good behavioral objectives.

Evaluation:

So that given an opportunity to write five minimum levels and five desired level behavioral objectives, all of the workshop participants will write at least four correctly stated objectives in each of the behavioral categories which will include the three communication checks of the goals and the appropriate E-1 and E-2 evaluation components.

Critique:

(a) E-1—to write five minimum level and five desired level behavioral objectives is the performance.

(b) E-2—"all of the workshop participants" is the teacher expectancy. "To write at least four correctly stated objectives in each of the behavioral categories" is the student requirement.

(c) Optional statement—which will include the three communication checks of the goals and appropriate E-1 and E-2 evaluation component is an optional statement to clarify the E-2.

(d) Classification—desired level behavioral.

Writing behavioral objectives, and evaluation components in particular, is an activity that requires careful planning and clear thinking. Perfection is never really anticipated or expected, but improvement in the stating and restating of behavioral objectives is highly desirable and should be strived for. The two primary parts of the evaluation component, referred to as E-1 and E-2, require the statement of an evaluation activity and the criterion by which the level of success in obtaining the intended goal can be determined. The use of the teacher expectancy part of the E-2 criterion statements can be omitted when it is not desirable or in the event it serves no particular purpose. However, the student requirement or success level must be included if the objective is to be classified as a desired level behavioral objective.

The difference between the minimum level behavioral and desired level behavioral refers to whether or not the objective statement was able to include an appropriate and desirable E-2 or criterion standard. It is always preferable to write at the desired level if possible, but only if the criterion standard is appropriate and provides more meaningful data for discovering the truth. A rule-of-thumb check for how well the evaluation statement communicates to its intended audience might be for a teacher to ask himself the following question: *If I were absent from class during the period of time that my objective is being evaluated, could some outside person who is unfamiliar with my course and objectives conduct the evaluation satisfactorily in my absence?* This naturally assumes the materials, equipment, and other necessary essentials are available.

A final note of caution is that the E-1 and E-2 components do not need to be stated entirely separate from each other. They may overlap or even be found scattered throughout the total evaluation statement. The important consideration is for the total evaluation statement to communicate a clear message. It is important for the E-1 and E-2 to be included in the total statement, but the self-check of these components or their relationship to each other in regard to word choice is purely a secondary consideration provided the total statement communicates a clear message.

An example of overlapping E-1 and E-2 components can be illustrated by reference to the seventh example previously critiqued. The total evaluation statement is as follows: "So that when given two weeks instruction on the flutophone, (75% of the children can *sight-read* without error) *a form measure exercise devised by the teacher* that includes only those notes taught during the instructional program." In this example the behavioral activity or E-1 to be required of the students is to sight-read a form measure exercise devised by the teacher. These words are italicized. The success level or E-2 component has been placed in parentheses: 75% of the children can sight-read without error. "Seventy-five percent" is the teacher expectancy, and "without error" is the student requirement. Both the E-1 and E-2 components include "sight-read," which in this instance is referred to as an overlapping term.

Chapter 5

COMPLETING THE WRITING PROCESS

If well thou hast begun, go on; it is
the end that crowns us, not the fight.
—Herrick

OBJECTIVE

The objective of this chapter is for the reader to become skillful in recognizing the component parts of behavioral and specific noninstructional objectives as determined by the achievement of a score of 85 percent or more on the following written examination.

A. On each of the following behavioral objectives place a slash mark (/) after the last word in the goal statement, underscore the E-1 with one line, and place parentheses around the E-2:

   1. To develop the skill of Algebra I students to evaluate scientific formulas as measured by a teacher-made written test of 20 questions such that 90% of the students can answer correctly 80% of the questions.

   2. To improve accuracy of using basic mathematical skills of fifth- and sixth-grade students as measured by a timed written test of 25 number-fact problems on which students should complete accurately 90% of all the problems in 10 minutes.

   3. To improve the performance of striking the home row keys for students taking Typing I so that during a one-minute timed

writing 90% of the students will be able to type 3½ lines of home row drills without error.

4. For fifth-grade science students to gain the ability to name the parts of the eye as measured by their ability to correctly answer 80% of the questions on teacher-made written examinations.

5. To increase eighth-grade history students' knowledge of the discovery and exploration of America as determined by a teacher-made test in which 80% of the students can identify the important explorers and the lands that they claimed for their country with 75% accuracy.

6. To develop the ability of eighth-grade students to change percents to decimals as measured by a teacher-made test of 20 questions on which 75% of the students will score 80% or better.

7. To develop seventh-grade general music students' note-reading recognition as measured by teacher-made tests so that by the end of the first semester 75% of the students will be able to read without error simple rhythm patterns.

8. To develop machine-wood safety habits in all woodworking students at BJHS as determined by written teacher-made safety tests on which 100% of the students score 85% or more.

9. To assist eleventh-grade science students in gaining a workable knowledge of and skill in writing chemical equations so that when given a written teacher-made test of 20 questions 75% of the students will score 80% or better correct answers.

10. To develop in junior high art students an awareness of van Gogh's style of painting so that when given a written test involving the viewing of 25 slides, 10 of which are van Gogh's, 90% of the students will score at least 6 out of 10 correct answers.

11. To improve the understanding of the present tense of verbs by first-year Spanish students as determined by a teacher-made test prepared from the text being used on which each student will achieve a minimum score of 80%.

12. To develop appreciation and understanding of Italian sixteenth-century paintings and knowledge of paintings and artists in a high school humanities class to be measured by the Rheims-Mashinga standardized art identification test on which all students will correctly identify 85% of the paintings.

13. To develop ability of trigonometry students to state values of trigonometric functions for specified arcs as measured by a written teacher-made test, with 85% of the students correctly answering 20 of 25 questions.

14. For bookkeeping students to understand the relationship of debits and credits in relation to increase and decrease in account

balances as determined by both teacher-prepared and standard textbook tests on which 90% of the students score 70% or better on both tests.

15. Students in American history will get a good understanding of the first 10 Amendments to the Federal Constitution as measured by a written teacher-made test, with the expectations that 75% of students will make 75% or more.

16. To improve reading comprehension skills of students in seventh-grade special reading classes as determined by the Stanford Diagnostic Reading Test, Form W, using the grade-equivalent score. It is expected that 80% of the students will measure a gain of three grade levels by the end of the school year.

17. To improve the ability of twelfth-grade English students to punctuate sentences effectively so that from a list of 50 teacher-constructed sentences, 90% of the students will be able to punctuate correctly 45 sentences.

18. To improve the knowledge of twelfth-grade English students concerning the vocabulary of literature as determined by a teacher-made written test on which each student must correctly define 40 out of 50 literary terms.

19. To develop the ability of ninth-grade algebra students to identify and solve first-degree equations of one variable as determined by a teacher-constructed test on which the majority of the students can correctly identify and solve 18 out of 20 problems.

20. To improve soccer skills in a ninth-grade physical education class, for a six-week unit, as measured by a teacher-made skills test with 75% of the class having a score of 85% or better.

21. To develop the ability to solve quadratic equations by Algebra II students as determined by 90% of the students successfully solving 80% of the problems on a teacher-made test.

22. To improve the achievement and skill of tenth-grade students in operating a compound microscope as determined by teacher observation and verbal questioning so that after 2 hours of instruction, 90% of the students will be able to correctly focus on an object using a 4 x lens, a 10 x lens, and a 40 x lens.

23. To increase the ability of eleventh-grade English students to write effective expository paragraphs as measured by their classroom writing of paragraphs using four specific methods of development according to standards set up in Warriner's Handbook, with 85% of the students demonstrating proficiency in writing paragraphs of definition, comparison, reasons, and details, so that ideas are communicated effectively and interestingly, according to the teacher's judgment.

24. To increase the eighth-grade students' ability to compute with rational numbers in mathematics as measured by a written objective appraisal test constructed by the classroom teacher in which 75% of the students will answer correctly 35 out of 50 problems.

25. To increase the efficiency in shooting the jump shot of varsity basketball players by having all players shoot the jumper from 20 feet away from the basket and being successful with 7 of 10 shots attempted.

26. To improve the speaking skills of seventh-grade students by increasing their vocabulary as determined by teacher appraisals of a 3-minute recitation, with 80% of the students making less than five errors in word choice.

B. On each of the following specific noninstructional objectives place a slash mark (/) after the last word in the goal statement, underscore the basic evaluation statement with one line, and indicate the quality criteria reference, if any, with parentheses:

1. To provide instruction in language arts, math, and science that is in keeping with the interest and level of achievement of students identified as underachievers so that when given written standardized tests based upon the objectives of language, arts, math, and science, there is a positive compliance in each area with at least 90% of these objectives and a positive correlation between the student interest and achievement as determined by teacher observations.

2. To develop for each grade level a program at the mathematical maturity level of the students and emphasizing the four basic number systems with the properties of each contrasted with the other postulated systems. Given a written achievement test and a set of pre-established criteria for determining the adequacy of the programs' technical concerns, 75% of the students will score 80% or above in achievement, attesting to the adequacy of the program with reference to maturity level of the students, and a competent math authority will find each of the pre-established criteria correctly met, attesting to its technical excellence.

C. Construct a unique specific noninstructional objective concerning any topic of your own interest. The objective can refer to nonlearner-oriented products, educational processes, facilities, or any other non-learner-oriented program variable. Place a slash mark (/) at the end of the goal statement, underscore the basic evaluation component, and place parentheses around the quality criteria.

(Answers follow bibliography at the end of the book.)

THE PROCESS APPROACH

The total process of writing behavioral objectives, including all component parts of goal statements and evaluation activities, may best be understood by defining three levels for the development of behavioral objectives. These levels, outlined in sequential order, may be seen in the following examples:

Goal statement (nonbehavioral). This consists of the basic goal statement and a check for communication. It is therefore a type of specific objective in which no evaluation is specified, and it is illustrated by the following statement:

> To increase the speed and improve the endurance
> of eighth-grade male students.

Minimum level behavioral. This level consists of the goal statement plus the E-1 evaluation statement, but does not include the E-2 success level criterion. It is illustrated as follows:

> To increase the speed and improve the endurance
> of eighth-grade male students as determined
> by their performance in running one mile.

Desired level behavioral. This level consists of the goal statement level plus both the E-1 and E-2 evaluation components. An example is as follows:

> To increase the speed and improve the endurance
> of eighth-grade male students so that given
> a stopwatch and an official, measured 440-yard
> track, the students will run one mile in less
> than 6 minutes by the end of the school year.

Casual observation of the three stated levels reveals that the goal statement level is the statement of a specific objective that defines a goal and includes the communication check, but indicates no end performance. It must therefore be considered as nonbehavioral. The minimum level behavioral objective states the goal and an end behavior, making it a behavioral objective, but does not place any particular standard upon the end performance to make it unique or distinctive. The desired level behavioral or instructional level objective clearly identifies the goal and the specific end behavior desired, and includes definite criterion to raise the standard of achievement to the level expected.

In this desired level behavioral example, the complete goal is "to increase the speed and improve the endurance of eighth-grade male students." The E-1 performance or evaluation activity expected of the students as an end product of the physical fitness improvement is "the students will run one mile." The optional statement in E-1 includes "so that given a stopwatch and an official, measured 440-yard track." The E-2 expected success level is "in less than 6 minutes," and the E-2 optional statement refers to "by the end of the school year." Thus, the evaluation measurement to be used will be to require all students, which now becomes an implied teacher expectancy, to run a distance of one mile at the completion of the program, using a stopwatch to record their time. The objective is achieved if all of the students can run one mile in less than 6 minutes; it is not achieved if some students fail to run the mile in the required time limit. This last requirement was added by the raising of the standard of achievement through the addition of the E-2 criterion statement.

Depending upon the value judgment of the instructor, there are several ways in which this objective could have been stated. One possible alternative is as follows:

1. *Goal statement (nonbehavioral):* To increase the speed and improve the endurance of eighth-grade male students.
2. *Minimum level behavioral:* To increase the speed and improve the endurance of eighth-grade male students as determined by their performance in running one mile.
3. *Desired level behavioral:* To increase the speed and improve the endurance of eighth-grade male students so that given a stopwatch and an official, measured 440-yard track, 80% of the students will run one mile in less than 6 minutes by the end of the school year.

This time the eighth-grade physical education instructor took into consideration that it might be physically impossible for all students to be able to run a mile in 6 minutes; thus the objective was unreal. Not wanting to lower his standard of achievement, he made allowance for the fact that 20 percent of the students could never reach the goal and stated his behavioral objective in meaningful terms as he saw it. At a later date this instructor might decide to lower his standard of achievement to 7 minutes since it is quite possible that 6 minutes is too fast for almost all eighth-grade students. *Since objectives are intended to pro-*

mote levels of accomplishment rather than to create failures, each one should be stated in realistic terms so there is a good chance that they will be successfully accomplished.

It is obvious that the criterion standards set forth in the E-2 part of evaluation (teacher expectancy and pupil level of success) will be based upon individual value judgments of the teachers. Thus, many times these criterion statements will not be appropriate for a particular group of students. In these instances the teacher should be flexible and should restate the criterion for the specific group or individual concerned.

Additional examples, without involving any rationale for value judgments, are stated as follows:

1. *Goal statement (nonbehavioral):* To improve the math skills of fourth-grade students in adding unlike fractions.
2. *Minimum level behavioral:* To improve the math skills of fourth-grade students in adding unlike fractions, as determined by Gores Test of fractions.
3. *Desired level behavioral:* To improve the math skills of fourth-grade students in adding unlike fractions, as determined by Gores Test of fractions, so that out of 25 additional problems, 80% of the students get at least 21 out of 25 answers correct.

Another example of stating an objective at different levels:

1. *Goal statement (nonbehavioral):* To train students in vocational electronics to understand the function and be able to make use of all components of a television set.
2. *Minimum level behavioral:* To train students in vocational electronics to understand the function and be able to make use of all components of a television set so that, given all of the correct parts necessary, they can construct a television set.
3. *Desired level behavioral:* To train students in vocational electronics to understand the function and be able to make use of all components of a television set so that, given all of the correct parts necessary, including a schematic diagram and tools, students can construct a television set and have it operating satisfactorily, according to the subjective judgment of the instructor, in less than eight class periods.

A third example of stating objectives at different levels:

1. *Goal statement (nonbehaviorial):* To increase the ability of students to solve algebra problems.
2. *Minimum level behavioral:* To increase the ability of students to solve problems in algebra as determined by a written standardized algebra test.
3. *Desired level behavioral:* To increase the ability of students to solve problems in algebra as determined by a written standardized algebra test in which the student obtains at least 80 correct answers out of 100 problems he is given to solve (or 80% correct answers).

Finally, four additional examples using widely differing areas and/or levels of instruction are as follows:

1. *Goal statement (nonbehavioral):* For kindergarten students to gain the ability to identify various animals.
2. *Minimum level behavioral:* For kindergarten students to gain the ability to identify various animals as determined by their ability to orally identify animals shown on a picture chart.
3. *Desired level behavioral:* For kindergarten students to gain the ability to identify various animals so that given a picture chart of 50 animals, 90% of the students will be able to correctly identify orally 75% of the animals.

• • •

1. *Goal statement (nonbehavioral):* To improve the written communication skill of sixth-grade pupils.
2. *Minimum level behavioral:* To improve the written communication skill of sixth-grade pupils as determined by their ability to write a sensible, decipherable paragraph.
3. *Desired level behavioral:* To improve the written communication skill of sixth-grade pupils as determined by their ability to write a sensible, decipherable paragraph on which 90% of the pupils use complete, non–run-on sentences with correct verb usage and not more than two misspelled words.

• • •

1. *Goal statement (nonbehavioral):* To develop typewriting skills of Vocational Office Education students.
2. *Minimum level behavioral:* To develop typewriting skills of

Vocational Office Education students as determined by the Standard Civil Service Typing Test.

3. *Desired level behavioral:* To develop typewriting skills of Vocational Office Education students so that given 540 hours of instruction, 80% of the students will type at 50 words per minute with no more than five errors as determined by the Standard Civil Service Typing Test.

•   •   •

1. *Goal statement (nonbehavioral):* To improve the offensive line-blocking skills of ninth-grade football players.
2. *Minimum level behavioral:* To improve the offensive line-blocking skills of ninth-grade football players as determined by the subjective opinion of the coach after watching each player perform 10 line blocks.
3. *Desired level behavioral:* To improve the offensive line-blocking skills of ninth-grade football players so that given the opportunity for each player to make 10 line blocks, 75% of the players will block correctly an assigned defensive player at least five times.

None of the objectives stated as examples in this chapter is artificial. Each was developed by classroom teachers or administrators after approximately six hours of workshop training in the techniques of writing behavioral objectives, as outlined in this book. In most instances the stated objectives represent the first writing efforts of the person involved. Undoubtedly none of the objectives is as good as it could be. In fact, it is a real challenge for any teacher, program planner, or project director to revise and restate behavioral objectives to the point that there is no doubt concerning their appropriateness, clarity, or specificity. The distinguishing characteristics in each of the behavioral objectives stated at the desired level is that they specify a goal, a behavior to be performed at the end of the project, and some standards to evaluate the quality of the performance that will be acceptable as proof that the objective has been achieved.

Frequently a difficult part of writing the complete behavioral objective occurs with language usage when connecting the statement of the goal to the statement of evaluation. Terms such as "as measured by," "when given the necessary variables," "as determined by whatever is appropriate in a particular objective," or the specification of other needed or desirable conditions may be clues that will be helpful.

SPECIFIC NONINSTRUCTIONAL OBJECTIVES

In Chapter 2 it was pointed out that there are two classifications of performance objectives. These classifications were shown to include behavioral objectives and specific noninstructional objectives. All of the discussion presented so far in this text has pertained to the development of behavioral objectives, which are generally considered to be the most useful for curriculum development and other instructional purposes. We will now focus our attention for the remainder of this chapter on understanding and writing specific noninstructional objectives.

The term "specific noninstructional objective" as developed in this text means a performance objective that is not primarily learner-oriented. It may frequently be considered as product-oriented. Product, in this sense, never pertains to the learner, but refers to the production of materials, equipment, facilities, and so on. The process objectives referred to in Accreditation Standards for Florida Schools would be typical of some objectives that would fit into the "specific noninstructional objective" category, and they will be useful for purposes of illustration.

Specific noninstructional objectives may be considered as lower level performance objectives when compared to minimum and desired level behavioral objectives. Figure 3 is an extension of Figure 2 (p. 17) and shows the differences in the three levels of performance objectives. Figure 3 reveals that the only requirements necessary for placing "specific noninstructional objectives" into the performance objective classification are (1) a distinct nonlearner-oriented goal specifying a clearly identified program variable and (2) a basic evaluation statement that specifies the performance or method by which the intended goal will be evaluated. It is not possible to check goals in this classification of objectives for the three communication checks used in minimum and desired level behavioral objectives. This is because no direct learner is involved, which also eliminates the use of the implied behavioral domain.

The basic statement of evaluation is closely related to and serves the same purpose as the E-1 evaluation statement used in behavioral objectives. It specifies the type of evaluation activity that will be used to determine whether or not the intent of the goal has actually been achieved. In some instances there will be no standards available or applicable for use as a quality criterion. In such cases they are not necessary. Quality criteria should be utilized, however, whenever it is available, practical, and appropriate.

PERFORMANCE OBJECTIVES

Specific Noninstructional Objectives	Behavioral Objectives	
I.	II. Minimum Level	III. Desired Level
Open- or Closed-Ended	Open-Ended	Closed-Ended

A. Goal
  1. Basic statement
    (a) Goal statement must identify a program variable that is nonlearner-oriented. Will usually refer to a nonlearner-oriented product, process, finance, structure, etc.
	A. Goal
	  1. Basic statement
	  2. Communication check:
	    (a) learner
	    (b) program variable
	    (c) implied behavioral domain
		A. Goal
		  1. Basic statement
		  2. Communication check:
		    (a) learner
		    (b) program variable
		    (c) implied behavioral domain

B. Evaluation
  1. Basic statement of performance or method of evaluation
	B. Evaluation
	  E-1. Performance, activity, behavior, or instrumentation
	    (a) optional statements
		B. Evaluation
		  E-1. Performance, activity, behavior, or instrumentation
		    (a) optional statements

2. Quality criterion to check standards if available.		E-2. Expected success level or criterion (a) optional statements

Figure 3. Performance Objective Levels and Components

Goals

Examples of goal statements used in specific noninstructional objectives are as follows:

1. To give each student the *opportunity to obtain counseling services.*

Critique:
(a) Program variable—"opportunity to obtain counseling services."
(b) Type—educational process objective.
2. For all cooperative training students *to be placed in appropriate training agencies.*
Critique:
(a) Program variable—"to be placed in appropriate training agencies."
(b) Type—educational process objective.
3. To develop *a logical and reasonable written plan of scope and sequence of mathematical skills* to ensure continuous growth for all children and to be implemented by each teacher.
Critique:
(a) Program variable—"a logical and reasonable written plan of scope and sequence of mathematical skills."
(b) Type—nonlearner-oriented educational product objective. Also implies educational process, but "a written plan" is the product in this instance.
4. To establish *an accredited learning laboratory* in Johnson Junior High School.
Critique:
(a) Program variable—"an accredited learning laboratory."
(b) Type—nonlearner-oriented educational facility or structure objective. Developing a "learning laboratory" is the facility.
5. For 50 percent of the classes in all Florida public schools at any given time *to reflect conditions or instances of behavior consistent with one-half or more of the statements listed on page 74, Standard 9.645, 4(9-a) of the Accreditation Standards for Florida Schools, 1969–70.*
Critique:
(a) Program variable—"to reflect conditions or instances of behavior."
(b) Type—educational process objective.

Evaluation

The evaluation components for specific noninstructional objectives are joined onto the goal statements in the same manner as in behavioral objectives. For the purposes of the present illustration, the goals will be restated and then the evaluation component for each one will be stated, followed by an evaluation critique. As in the case with other examples in this text, each goal and evaluation statement is a practical one that was written and is being used by one or more teachers in Florida.

Four of the five objectives were originally developed from the Accreditation Standards for Florida Schools, 1969–70. The examples shown were not chosen for their quality or correctness. In fact, two of them, if taken out of context, could be very questionable. However, they do represent practical illustrations of specific noninstructional objectives that have distinct basic statements of their intended goals and intended evaluation methods.

1. *Goal:*
   To give each student the opportunity to obtain
   counseling services.
   Evaluation:
   So that given the opportunities to participate in assembly
   programs, testing programs, career days, and to read the
   student handbook and daily bulletin, the student can identify
   the procedure for obtaining this service by his reaction on
   a written multiple-choice student survey instrument administered
   to a sample of homeroom groups representing one homeroom
   for each grade level.
   Critique:
   (a) Basic statement of method—identify on a written
       multiple-choice survey instrument.
   (b) Quality criteria—none.

2. *Goal:*
   For all cooperative training students to be placed in
   appropriate training agencies.
   Evaluation:
   So that given a list of eligible students and the names of
   all qualifying training agencies, the name of each student
   can be matched with an appropriate training agency that
   accepted his or her services.
   Critique:
   (a) Basic statement of method—matching a list of student
       names with a list of appropriate training agencies.
   (b) Quality criteria—each student or 100% must be
       placed with a training agency.

3. *Goal:*
To develop a logical and reasonable written plan of scope and sequence of mathematical skills and understandings to ensure continuous growth for all children and implemented by each other.
Evaluation:
So that when given the fully developed written plan, each of three qualified and impartial consultants will adjudge the plan to meet all of the stated requirements.
Critique:
(a) Basic statement of method—subjective judgment of three consultants based upon criteria they are given for evaluation of the plan.
(b) Quality criteria—"each consultant is to meet all of the stated requirements or criteria" implies 100% accomplishment.

4. *Goal:*
To establish an accredited learning laboratory in Johnson Junior High School.
Evaluation:
So that given a qualified learning laboratory consultant from the State Department of Education on a checklist of all the criteria for accrediting junior high school learning laboratories, the consultant will record in writing that each of the necessary criteria on the checklist has been adequately accounted for.
Critique:
(a) Basic statement of method—state consultant will use checklist to check the laboratory for accreditation purposes.
(b) Quality criteria—"each of the criteria being adequately accounted for" implies 100% acceptance.

5. *Goal:*
For 50 percent of the classes in all Florida public schools at any given time to reflect conditions or instances of behavior consistent with one-half or more of the statements listed on page 74, Standard 9.645, 4(a-d) of the Accreditation Standards for Florida Schools, 1969–70.
Evaluation:
As determined by written recordings of all instructional staff members at three different observational periods on a checklist developed from Standard 9.645, 4(a-d).

Critique:
(a) Basic statement of method—three written recordings on a checklist.
(b) Quality criteria—none, but goal statement implies a standard of 50% or more.

Chapter 6

UNIQUE WRITING PROBLEMS

There is no law of progress. Our future is in our own hands, to make or to mar. It will be an uphill fight to the end, and would we have it otherwise? Let no one suppose that evolution will ever exempt us from struggles.
—William Ralph Ingle

OBJECTIVE

The objective of this chapter is to develop in the reader an understanding of some of the problems that may be encountered in writing behavioral objectives, as determined by his scoring 85 percent correct answers on the following True–False examination.

1. Write true or false in the space provided for each question.

   (a) The choice of verbs is particularly important in goal statements. (a)_____

   (b) Some verbs communicate better and show more action than do others. (b)_____

   (c) Usually verbs identified by users of the goals-approach writing technique need to stand alone to convey their meaning. (c)_____

   (d) It may be possible to overemphasize verb usage in writing behavioral objectives. (d)_____

(e) For users of the goals-approach behavioral   (e)_____
objective writing technique, the selection
of verbs that are commonly acceptable
by most people without definition will be
adequate in most instances.

(f) Guidelines for checking the adequacy of   (f)_____
behavioral objective statements will probably
not be needed if the instructions for writing
behavioral objectives given in the goals
approach are adhered to rigidly.

(g) The two basic techniques for writing   (g)_____
objectives in behavioral terms are the
goals and the outcomes approaches.

(h) The evaluation requirement for both   (h)_____
behavioral objective writing techniques
is basically the same.

(i) It is easier to write behavioral objectives   (i)_____
for groups than for individuals.

(j) It is easier to write behavioral objectives   (j)_____
for long-range planning by the unit approach
rather than by the individual skill method.

(k) The goals-approach technique for writing   (k)_____
behavioral objectives is equally as effective
for writing in the cognitive, affective, and
psychomotor domains.

(l) Any objective stated for a group can be   (l)_____
modified and stated for an individual.

(m) Adapting behavioral objectives from   (m)_____
groups to individuals or individuals to
groups requires a change in the type of
evaluation performance stated in the E-1.

(n) The two basic ways to change an objective   (n)_____
in the cognitive domain from one type of
student to another are to change the success
level and the level of cognitive understanding.

(o) Unit objectives will usually include many   (o)_____
individual skills that must be accounted
for by the behavioral statement.

(p) Behavioral objectives based upon individual   (p)_____
skills taken from a skills continuum are
usually used for purposes of long-range
planning.

(q) Redundancy is a common problem inherent   (q)_____
to all behavioral objective development.

(r) Writing behavioral objectives by the individual skills approach will help to eliminate
redundancy.

(r)_____

(s) A good way to clarify objectives and to
avoid redundancy is to change either the
wording or the manner in which the evaluation components are joined onto the goal
statement.

(s)_____

(t) The psychomotor domain is the toughest
area in which to develop evaluation statements to be used in behavioral objectives.

(t)_____

(Answers follow bibliography at the end of the book.)

THE USE OF VERBS

In the statement of evaluation, many words are too general or open to
too many interpretations to be considered as the best alternative for
communicating the real intent of the measurement prescribed. The *word
"choice" is not so important in the statement of the goal,* since the basic
requirement is that the goal statement convey meaningful information
in a reasonably well-stated manner. *An entirely different situation arises
when words are selected for the evaluation component.*

*The major point of concern is whether or not certain words com-
municate better than others. Obviously they do.* Such words or verbs
according to Webster (1965) are typically full of "descriptive meaning
and characterizing quality, but are sometimes nearly devoid of these."
Thus, we need to use a behavioral verb that will indicate or give the
best description of the performance expected from the learner in any
given situation.

It could be helpful to identify and define all behavioral verbs in
the English language that appear to be usable in the construction of
behavioral objectives. Obviously, communication among the users of
words defined by common definitions would be better than with non-
users of such behavioral verbs. The merit, however, that might be found
in such an undertaking would probably apply mostly to theory and not
to practice. The task of completing such a statement of words would
be formidable, but to get people to study and memorize the words and
their definitions would be either impossible or at least impractical.

In actual usage *most verbs or activities identified by users of the
writing technique found in this text seldom needs to stand alone; that*

is, they are not used in isolation in the development of E-1 statements. For example, we might indicate in one instance that a student will take a "written examination." In this case the reading audience knows that the student will be involved in a writing activity. Another person might have stated in the same example that the student will take a "standardized examination." Again the reading audience knows that the student will be involved in a writing activity. Both examples might have been improved if they had stated that the student will take a "written standardized examination." This statement might also specify the particular name and battery of the standardized test.

The idea is that teachers should communicate the intent of their evaluation so that someone who is unfamiliar with that particular subject area or class could come in, during the teacher's absence, and evaluate the class by merely reading the information stated in the behavioral objective. This assumes that the necessary evaluation givens, conditions, and materials are available. If the choice of the right verb is the only way this communication can be attained, then the right verb should be used. If the mere identification of instrumentation will accomplish the same task, then the instrumentation can be used.

Emphasis should be placed upon verb usage, but not overemphasis. Probably all that is necessary is for the teacher to use behavioral verbs that appear to be commonly acceptable by most persons without definition. If there is a choice of more than one such verb, the one that seems to communicate best the desired behavior should be used. Then by clearly relating the verb to the other component parts of the evaluation statement, little doubt will remain concerning the appropriateness of the message.

GUIDELINES FOR DEVELOPMENT OF OBJECTIVES

There are a few simple guidelines that can be stated and used as criteria in determining the appropriateness or adequacy of any behavioral objective that may be stated. The relative worth of each objective developed can be roughly evaluated as being acceptable if the program planner or teacher can aswer "yes" to all of the following questions:

1. Is the problem area or goal that has been identified real, important, and practical?
2. Is the goal of the objective clearly stated so that it can be satisfactorily checked for the three communication variables?

3. Does the goal statement truly represent the original problem or need that was observed or prescribed?
4. Is it possible to gather the type of data that has been specified in the evaluation?
5. Can the E-1 performance or instrumentation that has been identified in the evaluation be accepted as clear evidence that the objective has either achieved or failed to achieve its goals?
6. Are the E-2 (expected success level and teacher expectancy standards) meaningful in regard to the type of data being collected and the proposed later analysis of this information?
7. Have all of the optional statements necessary for communication been inserted into the evaluation components of the objective?
8. If I were absent from school, could someone unfamiliar with my class, course content, and teaching techniques evaluate my students with only my behavioral objective statements for guidelines, assuming the necessary givens, conditions, and special considerations were all accounted for?

Any behavioral objective writer who has followed completely the writing techniques and instructions given in this text should have no difficulty in affirmatively answering each of these questions.

DIVERSIFYING THE WRITING PROCESS

Currently in the United States there are several different techniques being employed to write behavioral objectives. Briefly stated, they can be classified into two basic groups. The first group includes those techniques that utilize the *goals approach*. The advocates of the goals approach require that behavioral objectives include goal statements as well as evaluation statements. Usually this distinction will be found in the basic definition used for behavioral objectives. The writing technique advanced in this text qualifies as one of the techniques based upon the goals approach.

The second group or classification can be referred to as the *outcomes approach*. Advocates of this technique usually define a behavioral objective in terms of anticipated educational outcomes without reference to distinct goal statements. This technique only requires that objectives be written as performance statements that serve as measures of evaluation, which are essentially the same as E-1 and E-2 statements.

The original goals are implied but not specifically specified. In many instances, objectives written by the outcomes approach become closed-ended or closed-loop objectives without clear distinction being made between behavioral and specific noninstructional objectives or between minimum level and desired level alternatives.

It is not the purpose of this chapter to discuss the advantages or disadvantages of the two different approaches or to attempt to make comparisons. It should be obvious to the readers of this text that the author favors the *goals approach* and believes its advantages far outweigh any shortcomings. The goals approach takes longer to learn, but it provides more information or offers more in return.

Questions concerning the diversification and/or flexibility of the goals-approach writing process will sometimes arise and should be dealt with without too much difficulty. The most common questions formulated by workshop participants and college students learning to write behavioral objectives by the goals approach for the first time are: (1) Can the process be used for writing behavioral objectives for individuals? (2) How do you write for different types of children? (3) How do you write for units of instruction rather than for individual skills? (4) How do you eliminate redundancy? (5) How do you write complex objectives that require more than one sentence or one paragraph to state? (6) Can the goals approach be used successfully for both cognitive and affective behaviors? The purpose of this chapter is to answer these questions and to give necessary illustrations.

RELATING OBJECTIVES TO BOTH INDIVIDUALS AND GROUPS
Any objective that can be stated for an individual can be modified for group purposes or to take care of special types of students. Conversely, behavioral objectives stated for special groups or types of students can be altered to refer to individual students. This is easily accomplished by changing the learner(s) identified in the goal *and altering the evaluation component, particularly the E-2, to reflect the change in learner emphasis.* An example of the changes required to convert a group objective to an individual objective is:

Group:
To improve the pronunciation and intonation of *French I students,* with maximum communication and comprehension based on a minimal vocabulary and basic structure, so that given a particular

dialogue with which to work and two weeks practice time, *75% of the students will achieve a score of 100* on a teacher-made oral comprehension test.

Individual:
To improve the pronunciation and intonation of *Sandra Jane Smith,* with maximum communication and comprehension based on a minimal vocabulary and basic structure, so that given a particular dialogue with which to work and two weeks practice time, she will achieve a score of 85 or above on a teacher-made oral comprehension test.

In the group objective the learners were identified as French I students and the E-2 evaluation component used 75 percent of the students for the teacher expectancy, with a student requirement of a score of 100. The individual objective identified one member of the class, Sandra Jane Smith, as the learner, and based her student requirement upon her own potential. The student requirement and the teacher expectancy are the same thing for objectives written for individual students.

The same type of illustration would apply for any group or special types of students. If we are working with Head Start children we will call the learners Head Start children and use program variables, implied behavioral domains, and evaluation components that are appropriate for each particular individual or group. In the cognitive domain there are two basic ways to change an objective from one type of student to another, in addition to changing the learner identified in the goal statement. (This applies to objectives written for both individuals and groups.) *First, we can change the success level (teacher expectancy and/or student requirement) specified for the objective. Second, we can state the objective at a different level of cognitive understanding.* A combination of the two changes can be still another method of making a behavioral objective more appropriate for the type of learner to be involved.

In mathematics we might expect the average and advanced students to have the same goal, do the same activities concerning common course work, and be evaluated by the same methods. But the percentage used for teacher expectancy and learner requirement will undoubtedly be higher for the advanced student than for the basic or average. In some other subject areas we might expect that the differences between the advanced and basic or average students would involve different activities and a different type of evaluation. Thus, objectives in this area may be stated at a higher cognitive level with or without any change in teacher expectancy or student requirement. The choice is that of the teacher responsible for developing the objective and should represent a careful attempt to meet the needs of all of the pupils both as individuals and as groups.

WRITING COMPLEX OBJECTIVES FOR UNITS OF INSTRUCTION

Two common approaches to writing behavioral objectives for curriculum development are (1) to write for individual skills designated by a skills continuum and (2) to develop objectives for entire units of work. *The unit approach involves writing an overall objective that includes many skill.* A good illustration of the two approaches, and one that will also reveal the relationships that may be found between the two, can be seen in the development of some objectives for a behavioral objective workshop as follows:

Individual Skills:
1. For workshop participants to increase their ability to write effective goal statements, as determined by 90% of the participants listing, without error, the names of each of the three major criteria that can be used as communication checks of a goal.
2. For workshop participants to understand the three levels for writing performance objectives, as measured by 95% of the participants orally naming correctly, as presented in this workshop, each of the three levels for writing objectives and relating each level, without error, to a particular type of objective also defined in this workshop.
3. To improve the workshop participants' skill in writing desired level behavioral objectives as determined by 80% of the workshop participants writing and making, without error, a critical analysis of one behavioral objective written at the desired level.

The three objectives could be considered as individual or basic skill objectives. *Teachers will tend to write objectives based upon components of a skills continuum when they are primarily concerned with developing objectives for daily activities. Unit objectives, which in many respects are better suited for overall curriculum development, represent a long-range–planning type of activity.* The following objective, which could be written for the same behavioral objective workshop as were the three individual examples, shows one method for organizing many skills into one unit objective.

Unit behavioral objective:
For workshop participants to increase their understanding of and technical skills in writing behavioral objectives, so that given a comprehensive written examination and a one-hour time limit, 90% of the participants completing the workshop will obtain a score of at least 75%. The activities specified on the examination are as follows:

1. *Identify in writing* the one word that best represents the chief concern in writing objectives in behavioral terms.
2. Correctly *write* the name of each of the two major component parts of a behavioral objective.
3. *Name and correctly summarize* in a brief statement of less than seventy-five words each of the three types of behavioral objectives as defined in the workshop.
4. *List,* without error, the names of each of the three major criteria that can be used as communication checks of a goal.
5. *Describe* separately, in correct but brief statements, each of the three distinct behavioral domain areas.
6. *Name* correctly, as presented in this workshop, each of the three levels for writing objectives and *relate* each level, without error, to a particular type of objective also defined in this workshop.
7. *Explain* in general terms and in less than fifty words the differences between behavioral objectives and procedures.
8. *Write* and *make a critical analysis,* without error, of one behavioral objective written at the minimum level.
9. *Write* and make a critical analysis, without error, of one behavioral objective written at the desired level.
10. *Create,* without error, from the words stated below, one well-*organized* desired level behavioral objective that is structurally correct with reference to communication checks of the goal and the use of E-1 and E-2 evaluation components and optional statements.

"to word of students when word section Stanford test that of students months 75% students at increase grade improve the study skills given the second grade so that study skills of the Reading Achievement Primary Battery I, pretest scores all the and nine of instruction of the will achieve least on of one level."

Close observation of this unit objective reveals that it not only includes the three objectives stated for individual skills, but in addition includes many other skills not covered by the individual objectives. Writing unit objectives saves much time in formulating, repeating, and checking goal statements. Another advantage is that the unit approach enables the teacher to do long-range planning of objectives that will require different understanding levels on the part of students. The sample unit behavioral objective stated requires cognitive behavior by students that ranges from simple knowledge or recall to the beginning of the development of understanding at the synthesis level.

In summing up the use of complex behavioral objective statements, we find that they will be most frequently utilized to (1) develop units of instruction based upon long-range planning, (2) avoid repetition of goal statements, and (3) avoid restricting the activities that may be necessary for meaningful evaluation. This latter point may become increasingly important in the development of E-1 components for objectives written at the minimum level in the affective domain.

PROBLEMS OF REDUNDANCY AND THE AFFECTIVE OR PSYCHOMOTOR DOMAIN

The problem of redundancy is more often than not imagined rather than real. If it occurs it will probably be due to carelessness by the writer rather than necessity inherent in any particular writing technique. There are times when repetition provides reinforcement or tends to make an objective communicate just a little better. In these instances no change is to be desired.

Writing objectives by the unit-method approach is one of the best ways to avoid redundancy in the development of goal statements. Sometimes one goal can be appropriate for the development of many skills. Whenever this is the case it is useless to repeat goal statements by writing out each objective individually.

Another way to avoid redundancy and to possibly aid in the clarification of some objectives is to change the manner in which goals are joined to the statements of evaluation. This can be accomplished by either a change in the connecting words or by a separation of some of the evaluation components from the body of the objective. Examples of this technique taken from two proposals developed for Title III funding are as follows:

1. To increase the reading achievement of first-grade students as measured by the total score obtained on the Stanford Reading Achievement test in which students obtain the following:
   (a) 25 percent decrease in the number of students entering the second grade who are one-half or more years behind grade level than in the previous year.
   (b) An average of 0.2 increase in the grade level achievement of students entering the second grade over the preceding year.

2. To help school personnel to: (1) become more willing to involve themselves socially and professionally in school, (2) perceive administration more positively, and (3) perceive the organizational climate of the school as being more open, more autonomous, and less controlled, as determined respectively by the following:
   (a) the Disengagement, Esprite, Intimacy, and Hindrance scales of the *Organizational Climate Description Questionnaire.*
   (b) the Openness, Autonomy, and Controlled scales of the *Organizational Climate Description Questionnaire.*

3. To assist students in the: (1) understanding of and skill in dealing with human behavior, (2) perception of the teacher as an individual whose work is helping pupils learn, (3) ability to take initiative in, or responsibility for, trying to work out some of their own simpler problems, (4) recognition that data from past studies can be an aid in understanding and appreciating the behavior of others, and (5) application of a causal approach to historical events and to current social problems as evaluated by:
   (a) *Social Causality Test* by Ralph H. Ojemann.
   (b) *Problems Situation Test* by Ralph H. Ojemann.

4. To improve the personal adequacy and instructional efficiency of classroom teachers so that given a fully developed comprehensive in-service training program and one year of program implementation, 85% of the teachers will successfully be performing the following activities:

(a) working in harmonious relationship with other faculty members on problems of common concern.
(b) developing written reports, project activities, and pupil analyses resulting from in-service training.
(c) increased teacher utilization of more innovative materials, equipment, and teaching techniques.
(d) writing more accurate and objective diagnosis procedures to determine both individual student needs and progress.

The success of these evaluation activities will be judged by an evaluation team that includes the building principal, county staff supervisors, and visiting teachers.

In these examples only the first and fourth objectives were written at the desired level. Objectives two and three specified only an E-1 but no E-2 criterions. Objective number four states a teacher expectancy (85%) which is part of an E-2, but cannot stand alone without the learner requirements of how successful each of the four activities must be. The activities belong to the E-1. Two of the objectives were written in the affective domain, which will attest to the usefulness of the goals-approach for writing in this area. The minimum level behavioral classification is particularly useful for writing many objectives in this domain, for the various reasons specified in Chapter 2. There are no problems presented by objectives in the psychomotor domain that would require any unique changes in the goals-approach method. In fact, *due to the ability to observe many overt behaviors in the psychomotor domain, it is in many respects the easiest of the three domains in which to write behavioral objectives by any approved technique.*

Chapter 7

GUIDELINES
FOR
WRITING
OBJECTIVES

A sound head, an honest heart, and a humble
spirit are the three best guides through time
and to eternity.
That man may safely venture on his way, who is
so guided that he cannot stray.
—Walter Scott

OBJECTIVE

The objective of this chapter is for students to be able to organize, plan, and construct their own behavioral objectives at the desired level using guideline materials, so that when given both types of guidelines and two identified needs, 85 percent of the students can develop two behavioral objectives with no more than one error for each guideline completed.

Note: The guideline materials and needs are illustrated on the following two pages. A maximum time allowance of 30 minutes will be considered sufficient for completing the guideline forms including the statement of each of the two behavioral objectives at the desired level. (The use of the process in filling out the guidelines will be evaluated rather than competency in the area involved in the objective.) Answers follow bibliography at the end of the book.

SELECTING OBJECTIVES

Seldom does the final choice of goals or objectives come easily. Frequently it will be necessary to sketch out some type of rough guideline

School Level _____

Subject Area _____   School _____

Page Number _____   Teacher _____

State Standard No. _____

BEHAVIORAL OBJECTIVE GUIDELINES

I. Delegated or Prescribed Need
    There is a need to develop more positive atti-
tudes among teachers toward in-service training
and instructional innovation.
_____
_____

II. Goal Statement (Communication Checks)
    A. Behavioral domain: _____
    B. Learner: _____
    C. Program variable: _____

III. Minimum Level Objective
    D. Combine A, B, and C (above) into goal state-
       ment:
_____
_____
_____

    E. Identify type of evaluation or measurement
       instrument:
_____
_____
_____

IV. Desired Level Objective
    F. Combine D and E (above) into a statement:
_____
_____
_____

    G. Identify and insert the success criteria or
       standards of how well the learner must achieve
       into F (above):
_____
_____
_____
_____

SYSTEMS PROGRAM PLANNING AND DEVELOPMENT CHART

NEEDS	GOALS	ACTIVITIES	EVALUATION MEASURES	EVALUATION SCHEDULE
The students were observed to have negative attitudes toward attending school and in their perception of teachers. Source: Type: Learner: Behavioral domain: Behavioral Objective				

from which the goals and later the behavioral objectives can be developed. It was established earlier that evaluation is based upon the statements of behavioral objectives. Behavioral objectives are based upon goals, and these in turn are based upon some observed need that existed prior to the statement of the goals. In other words, from the needs we state goals, from the goals we state performance objectives, and from the performance objectives we establish evaluation for specific units of the overall program.

The needs identified may be observed, prescribed, intuitive, or detected by a survey. Regardless of the source of the needs or how they were determined, they should be analyzed at the beginning of any program development activities. Possibly the most visible illustration of the necessity for analyses of needs is in their transformation to behavioral objectives. Many recent innovative programs that appeared to be well thought out and designated have ended up as failures due to poor goal identification and evaluation components in the objectives that do not relate to the needs of the program.

For example, we might consider any one of three different children who have been diagnosed as having problems relating to self-concept. First, we have the child who habitually tends to perform acts that we call aggressive behavior. He may do this through aggressive language, rebellion to authority, or some other overt action such as picking on another child. The second child exhibits overly submissive behavior. He is very unobtrusive and undemanding. He imitates others a lot and may in return be the object of their overly aggressive behavior. The third child is neither aggressive nor submissive but tends to withdraw completely from participation in his social environment.

In each of the preceding situations the child may be correctly diagnosed as having a self-concept problem. And in each instance the child could be administered an acceptable self-concept test and an attitude test prior to the beginning of correctional activities. At the end of the program the tests could again be administered and reveal in each instance that the child involved made significant positive change in self-concept; thus, the evaluation of the project would show that the program was a complete success.

However, further study of the three children by a qualified consultant could reveal that the first child was still overly aggressive, the second child still overly submissive, and the third child almost completely withdrawn. According to the consultant, the self-concept behavioral change program would have been a complete failure because the only behavioral changes that would be acceptable were, respectively, less aggression, reduced submission, and the development of a more outgoing behavior. In this instance the writer of the behavioral objectives was in error in allowing the evaluation statement to designate a paper-and-pencil test as a means of determining changes in behavior that were not measurable in such terms.

USE OF GUIDELINES

Table 1 is a form that was developed in Hillsborough County, Florida, for use with the Head Start and Special Reading teachers. This form was devised primarily as a means of developing competency in writing behavioral objectives, using the techniques taught in this text and applying them to the Accreditation Standards for Florida Schools.

The headings in Table 1 are self-explanatory. In Roman numeral I the prescribed standard or need is defined. This step may be omitted when such identification is deemed unnecessary. Roman numeral II enables the teacher to specify the three communication check factors necessary in the statement of the goal. These variables are pulled from the need or the state standard. In Roman numeral III-D the communication check variables are combined into a meaningful goal statement. In III-E the E-1 or performance activity or instrumentation is identified. Under Roman numeral IV-F the goal statement is combined with the E-1 to make a minimum level behavioral objective. In IV-G the E-2 (expected success level and teacher expectancy) is incorporated into the objective to bring it to the desired level behavioral status.

It is important to recognize that the complete guidelines are used only when a student or teacher is first learning this goals-approach to writing behavioral objectives. As soon as teachers become thoroughly familiar with the writing process, including the communication checks of the goals and both the E-1 and E-2 evaluation components, and are confident of their own competency to write behavioral objectives, they can leave off two or three of the guidelines.

The teachers for whom this guideline material was developed were writing behavioral objectives for State Accreditation Standards, the page number and state standard number were included in the heading. These components could be omitted from objectives that were based upon other types of needs.

Both guidelines I and II can be omitted if a teacher has her need firmly established in mind and has developed competency in developing

TABLE 1

Physical Education
<u>Subject Area</u>
<u>162</u>
Page Number
<u>(2)(a)1</u>
State Standard No.

Oakcrest Elementary
School Name and Level

<u>Mr. Max McKeown</u>
Teacher

BEHAVIORAL OBJECTIVE GUIDELINES

I. Delegated or Prescribed Need
  (2) Instruction
    (a) Scope of program (primary)
      1. Movement exploration: (X-level 1) Students have participated in programs of exploration of fundamental movements, some of which are: walking, running, jumping, hopping, leaping, skipping, sliding, galloping, bending, turning, twisting, swinging, pushing, pulling, throwing, catching, striking, and many combinations of these.

II. Goal Statement (Communication Checks)
  A. Behavioral domain: Psychomotor
  B. Learner: Grade one students
  C. Program variable: Fundamental locomotor and axile movements

III. Minimum Level Objective
  D. Combine A, B, and C (above) into goal statement: To improve the fundamental locomotor and axile movements of grade-one students.
  E. Identify type of evaluation or measurement instrument: Teacher-made test of locomotor and axile movements.

IV. Desired Level Objective
  F. Combine D and E (above) into a statement: To improve the fundamental locomotor and axile movements of grade-one students as determined by a teacher-made test of locomotor and axile movements.
  G. Identify and insert the success criteria or standards of how well the learner must achieve into F (above): To improve the fundamental locomotor and axile movements of grade-one students so that 80% of the students can perform correctly 75 % of all the locomotor and axile movements described in a teacher-made test.

Source: Behavioral Objective Guidelines, Table 1 contributed by Dr. Anita J. Harrow, Supervisor of Research, and Evaluation, Hillsborough County, Florida.

and preparing critiques of goal statements. A competent behavioral objective writer can perform only Roman numerals III and IV without sacrificing either the effectiveness of the communication or the quality of these objectives component parts. Experience has proved that teachers who become competent in utilizing this goals-approach to writing behavioral objectives and who do not find it necessary to write out the State Standards or otherwise use Roman numeral I and II can, with ease, develop several completely new behavioral objectives within one hour.

Tables 2 and 3 are additional examples of rough guidelines that show how behavioral objectives can be charted and developed for programs in which the specific needs and content have not already been prescribed. Tables 2 and 3 reveal how two behavioral objectives were actually developed for a research project in one of Florida's larger counties. The need in Table 2 was developed into a minimum level behavioral objective, whereas Table 3 was used to develop a desired level behavioral objective.

Tables such as 2 and 3 are used to identify only one problem or need. They are excellent devices upon which to record and store information obtained by direct observation, but can have equal value in identifying problems and needs developed from other sources. Necessary information is stored in this tabular form until it can be used later to write a behavioral objective. Both tables were developed through observation of the students and faculty members in three experimental schools over a two-month period. The needs column is used to record the needs or problems that are encountered. In addition it is used to identify how the need was established (source), the type of problem, the learner, and the behavioral trait or domain. It is not necessary that all of these variables be identified in the needs column, but since this information is readily available it would be a waste not to record it.

The way this table has been utilized most frequently is for teachers, researchers, or program developers to carry several blank forms of the table with them when they visit a school about which they are concerned. Usually several visits will be necessary before the observers are confident they have identified the salient problems or have properly diagnosed the needs. As soon as a definite problem or need has been determined, the observer will fill out the needs column. This will usually include a brief statement of the problem or need, the source or way it was obtained, the type, who the learner will be, and what behavioral trait or traits are primarily involved.

It does not make any difference whether the needs column is com-

TABLE 2

NEEDS	GOALS	ACTIVITIES	EVALUATION MEASURES	EVALUATION SCHEDULE
Poor interpersonal relationships among faculty members Source: Observed Type: Social-emotional Learner: Teachers Behavioral Trait: Affective	To improve staff interpersonal relations Selection: Real, important	Conduct weekly in-service training program using the "Human Development Relationship Improvement Program" developed by Jerome Barline and L. Benjamin Wycoff (published by the Human Development Institute of Atlanta, Ga.). The HDI is a programmed course for the teaching of improved interpersonal relations. It requires two people working together in constant interaction.	a. Comparison of prepost test changes in self-other scores of teacher/principal participants in the Pilot Demonstration Schools and Control Schools as measured by the Index of Adjustment and Values. b. Comparison of prepost test changes in scores of the Pilots Demonstration Schools and Control School facilities as measured by the Organizational Climate Description Questionnaire. c. Teacher Reaction Forms 1 and 1A SEL.	September and January

Behavioral Objective (Minimum Level)

To help teachers and administrators to: (a) deepen awareness of their own feelings and the feelings of others, (b) enhance appreciation of their own potentials, and (c) improve their attitudes towards the school environment as measured by the gains achieved in prepost test scores of the Index of Adjustment and Values and Organizational Climate Description Questionnaire and by data obtained from Teacher Reaction Forms 1 and 1A developed by SEL.

TABLE 3

NEEDS	GOALS	ACTIVITIES	EVALUATION MEASURES	EVALUATION SCHEDULE
1. To improve communication through verbal skills. 2. To improve auditory discrimination for certain sounds. 3. To improve classroom reading performance. 4. To increase vocabularies. Source: Observation and tests Type: Academic, content-reading Learner: Students Trait: Cognitive	To improve the reading achievement and skills of disadvantaged first-grade students.	Utilize the Open Court Publishing Co. Correlated Language Arts Program and Materials. The program and materials feature a complete teacher guide and lesson plans, intensive initial phonics, early writing reinforcements activities, readers utilizing children's classics, together with readers that are highly correlated to the total Language Arts Program, since the same words and stories are used in the development of reading, writing, and speech skills. Both matched group techniques and time studies will be employed. "After-test-only" technique was used in the experimental design.	Stanford Achievement Tests, Primary Battery 1, including measures of word reading, paragraph meaning, vocabulary, word study skills, and spelling.	May, 1965 May, 1966 May, 1967 May, 1968

Behavioral Objective (Desired Level)

To increase the reading achievement and skills of disadvantaged first-grade students as measured by the total score obtained on the Stanford Reading Achievement Test, Primary Battery 1, in which the student obtained the following: (a) a 25% decrease in the number of students entering the second grade who are one-half or more years behind grade level than was the case for the previous year and (b) an average of .3 increase in the grade level achievement of students entering the second grade over those of the preceding year.

pleted in the form of an identified problem or the statement of a need. Table 2 is an example of a completed form that stated a problem: "Poor interpersonal relationships among faculty members." This statement is definitely a problem, not a need. Table 3 identified problems and stated them as needs such as "to improve communication through verbal skills." Either way the column is completed will be sufficient to allow the observer to later complete the remaining portion of the form.

At any convenient later date the goals, activities, evaluation measures, and evaluation schedule columns are completed at the observer's own convenience. Usually the activities column is the last one to be filled in, and generally it follows the statement of the behavioral objective at the bottom of the page. This objective can be written any time after the needs, goals, and evaluation columns are completed. Information for the goals column is obtained from the need statements. It is not necessary that the goal statements be complete and checked for communication at the time they are first written, or that they be the same statement that will eventually be placed into the behavioral objective. Table 2 is an example of a goal statement that was later changed in the behavioral objective. Table 3 used the same goal statement in the behavioral objective that was stated in the goals column. Actually there need not be any hard and fast rules for using these charts or similar ones. Teachers should devise their own charts and utilization techniques based upon their needs and how the charts can best serve their purpose.

Anderson, Ronald D. "Formulating Objectives for Elementary Science (Part 1)," *Science and Children*, Vol. 5, No. 1, September 1967, pp. 20–23.

> The first of two articles on elementary science objectives. Examples are given showing how to formulate objectives for the elementary science curriculum as behavioral or performance objectives. A later article will deal with using meaningful objectives as a basis for evaluating the success of the teaching. The new AAAS program, "Science—A Process Approach," is discussed.

Atkin, J. Myron. "Behavioral Objectives in Curriculum Design. A Cautionary Note." Presented in February 1968 at the annual meeting of the American Educational Research Association in Chicago.

> Takes position that worthwhile goals are first in value, not methods for assessing progress toward goals.

Bloom, Benjamin, et al. *Taxonomy of Educational Objectives. Handbook I: Cognitive Domain*, New York: McKay, 1956.

> This system for classifying objectives has been used as a basis for many later studies.

Brothers, Aileen, and Holsclaw, Cora. "Fusing Behavior into Spelling," *Elementary English*, XLVI, No. 1, January 1969, pp. 25–28.
> Authors list five spelling behaviors in written work. Suggestions are made for devising new types of behavioral tests.

Caffyn, Lois. "Behavioral Objectives: English-Style," *Elementary English*, XLV, No. 8, December 1968, pp. 1073–1074.
> Author suggests the formulation of desired adult competencies in the four language arts areas in terms of what people do. Then identifies competencies for each grade level. Check each lesson for validity as it contributes to one or more of the long-range competencies. If it does not contribute to one or more of the long-range competencies, if it does not serve, probably it should be eliminated.

Colorado State Department of Education. *Some Behavioral Objectives for Elementary School Mathematics Program.* Denver, Colorado: State Department Publications, 1968.
> A guide for developing behavioral objectives, which includes samples of objectives.

FASCD Mailbag. *Behavioral Objectives: Pro and Con.* Tallahassee, Florida: Florida Association for Supervision and Curriculum Development, December 1968.
> Reprints of three papers which were presented in February 1968 at the annual meeting of the American Educational Research Association in Chicago.
>
> Atkins, J. Myron. "Behavioral Objectives in Curriculum Design: A Cautionary Note."
>
> Popham, W. James. "Probing the Validity of Arguments Against Behavioral Goals." Los Angeles, California: Vincet Associates, 1967.
>
> Raths, James D. "Specificity as a Threat to Curriculum Reform."

Florida State Department of Education. *Proposed 1968–1969 Accreditation Standards for Flroida Schools.* Tallahassee, Florida: Florida State Department of Education, 1968.
> These tentative standards have been written emphasizing student behavioral objectives.

Garvey, James F. "The What and Why of Behavioral Objectives," *The Instructor*, Vol. LXXXVII, No. 3, April 1968, p. 127.
> Simplified definition of behavioral objectives.

Grade Teacher, Vol. LXXXIV, April 1967.
> This volume contains a number of articles dealing with behavioral objectives as related to basic school subjects. Other parallel topics are also included.

Krathwahl, David R., et al. *Taxonomy of Educational Objectives. Handbook II: Affective Domain*. New York: McKay, 1956.
Second volume of Bloom and associates classification systems.

Mager, Robert F. *Developing Attitudes for Learning*. Palo Alto, California: Fearon, 1968.
Suggestions are made for assisting teachers in helping students have a favorable attitude toward a subject.

Mager, Robert F. *Preparing Instructional Objectives*. Palo Alto, California: Fearon, 1962.
Author has put together a programmed book on how to prepare objectives. The reader can self-instruct himself on the form of usefully stated objectives.

Mager, Robert F., and Beach, Kenneth M., Jr. *Developing Vocational Instruction*. Palo Alto, California: Fearon, 1967.
While this is planned primarily for vocational instruction, there are many suggestions pertinent to academic instructional objectives and criteria for evaluating them.

Mayor, John R. "Science and Mathematics in the Elementary School," *The Arithmetic Teacher*, Vol. 14, No. 8, December 1967, pp. 629–635.
Description of the AAAS program known as "Science—A Process Approach." In this program, objectives are carefully stated in terms of what the child is able to do or what one who observes the child can see him do. Instruments are provided for measurement. Shows the close relationship between mathematics and science at the elementary school level.

Oakleaf Elementary School. *Mathematics Continuum*. Pittsburgh, Pennsylvania: Baldwin-Whitehall School District publication.
Behavioral objectives for an elementary school program employing the levels and strands strategy.

Oakleaf Elementary School. *Behavioral Objectives for Reading*. Pittsburgh, Pennsylvania: Baldwin-Whitehall School District publication.
Behavioral objectives for an elementary school program employing the levels and strands strategy.

Ober, Richard L. *Theory into Practice Through Systematic Observation*. FERDC Research Bulletin, Vol. 4, No. I, Spring 1968. Florida Educational Research Development Council, 1968.
Descriptions of several systems of classroom observation, such as the Reciprocal Category System, the Teaching Practice Observation Record, the Florida Taxonomy of Cognitive Behavior.

Ojemann, Ralph H. "Should Educational Objectives Be Stated in Behavioral Terms?" *Elementary School Journal*, Vol. 68, No. 5, February 1968, pp. 223–231.
Author feels that objectives should be so stated, with the provision that

we recognize that the overt behavior in the classroom is not the same
as that in situations in which the individual is on his own. Seems to
feel that we should not neglect the objectives concerned with the significance of content to the individual.

Ojemann, Ralph H. "Should Educational Objectives Be Stated in Behavioral Terms?" Part II, *Elementary School Journal,* Vol. 69, No. 5, February 1969, pp. 229–235.
    Points out misuses in the practice of formulating objectives in behavioral
    terms. States that the purpose of doing so is to make objectives so mean-
    ingful that they can be used in communication. This may not be the only
    or best way of achieving meaningfulness, but appears to be the best
    method now available.

Plowman, Paul. *Behavioral Objectives Extension Service.* Chicago, Illinois:
Science Research Research Associates, 1968–69.
    A series of eight units on behavioral objectives, planned as teacher-growth
    handbooks. The emphasis is on measurable growth of teacher and stu-
    dent. An excellent bibliography is included in each unit.

    Unit I, Oct. 1, 1968. *Behavioral Objectives and Teacher Success.*
        Author lists characteristics of well-formulated behavioral objectives.
        Objectives are classified as academic, cognitive, creative, craftsman-
        ship, and leadership skills. Other units deal specifically with eight
        subject areas: who, what, and how we teach, and gauging growth
        and effectiveness.
    Unit II, Nov. 1, 1968. *Behavoral Objectives in English and Literature.*
    Unit III, Dec. 1, 1968. *Behavioral Objectives in Social Studies.*
    Unit IV, January 1, 1969. *Behavioral Objectives in Science.*
    Unit V, February 1, 1969. *Behavioral Objectives in Biology.*
    Unit VI, March 1, 1969. *Behavioral Objectives in Mathematics.*
    Unit VII, April 1, 1969. *Behavioral Objectives in Art and Music.*
    Unit VIII, May 1, 1969. *Behavioral Objectives in Reading.*

Popham, W. James. *"Selecting Appropriate Educational Objectives."*
Los Angeles, California: Vincet Associates, 1967.
    A series of seven filmstrips and seven recording tapes. "Systematic Instruc-
    tional Decision-Making" is an overview to the program.
    "Educational Objectives" is a program designed to develop one's ability
    to identify and write behavioral objectives.
    "Selecting Appropriate Educational Objectives" gives one practice in using
    modified versions of the *Taxonomy of Educational Objectives* developed
    by Bloom and associates.
    "Establishing Performance Standards" helps teachers identify student and
    class performance standards.
    "Appropriate Practice" is designed to assist the teacher with the selection
    of learning activities most likely to lead to successful attainment of goals.
    "Perceived Purpose" helps teachers establish learner interest in instruc-
    tional activities.

"Evaluation" deals with preassessment, test design, data interpretation, and teacher effectiveness based on student achievement.

"Probing the Validity of Arguments Against Behavioral Goals" gives answers to eleven reasons given by others in opposition to objectives stated in terms of measurable learner behaviors.

Raths, James D. "Specificity as a Threat to Curriculum Reform." Presented in February 1968 at the annual meeting of the American Educational Research Association in Chicago.

Asks for compromise. Seems to feel that the requirement for specificity advanced by some are in conflict with the values of teachers. Criteria needs to be developed that will allow teachers to write objectives in way that is more specific than now, and yet be congruent with their values.

Sanders, Norris M. *Classroom Questions: What Kind?* New York: Harper & Row, 1966.

A very fine volume related to educational objectives.

Simpson, Elizabeth Jane. "The Classification of Educational Objectives: Psychomotor Domain."

Explains five levels of levels of behavior in the psychomotor domain. It was developed through Research Project No. OE 5-85-104, University of Illinois, 1966. Dr. Simpson is now with the U.S. Office of Education in Washington, D.C., and expects to publish the final taxonomy document during 1970–1971.

Vincet Associates. *Educational Objectives.*

This is one of a set of combination tape-filmstrip packages. This filmstrip assists with the writing of behavioral objectives. A very basic treatment. Address: Vincet Associates, P.O. Box 24714, Los Angeles, California 90024. A second series has been released by Vincet, which is also related to objectives and curriculum design.

Webster, Merriam. *Webster's Seventh New Collegiate Dictionary:* Springfield, Massachusetts: G. C. Merriam Company, 1965, p. 986.

Wisconsin Department of Public Instruction. *K–6: Guidelines to Mathematics.* State Department publication, 1966.

A summary of examples of behavioral objectives for the elementary school.

Chapter 1 (Allow 10 points per question):
1. specifically defined objectives
2. (a) aid in curriculum planning
   (b) promote increased pupil achievement
   (c) improve the techniques and skills of program evaluation
3. behavioral objectives
4. specific noninstructional objectives
5. (a) in the classroom
   (b) for research
   (c) in proposal writing
   (d) for curriculum development activities
6. appropriate level
7. evaluation
8. procedures
9. technical knowledge, subject matter competency
10. goals

Chapter 2 (Value for each question is stated in test):

1. (a) True   (f) False
   (b) False   (g) True
   (c) True   (h) False
   (d) True   (i) True
   (e) True   (j) True

2. Definitions are not limited to, but should include, reference
   to the following information:
   (a) goal and evaluation components
   (b) identifies exact aim, purpose, or intent of the objective
   (c) identifies goal checked by three communication checks
       (or specifies learner, program variable, and implied
       behavioral domain) and in addition specifies evaluation
       instrumentation, performance, or activity
   (d) same as (c) or same as (e) minus the E-2 component or
       success level
   (e) same as (c) plus reference to E-2 or learner success level
   (f) performance objective that is not learner-oriented; could
       refer to product, facility, or process orientation of objective

3. (a) desired level   (f) desired level
   (b) desired level   (g) minimum level
   (c) desired level   (h) minimum level
   (d) minimum level   (i) desired level
   (e) desired level   (j) minimum level

Chapter 3 (Allow 20 points for each goal statement; exact word
            selection or usage not required):

1. *Critique:*
   (a) Learner—elementary school children.
   (b) Program variable—rhythmic movement or performing
       rhythmic movement to music.
   (c) Behavioral domain—psychomotor (skill in performing
       rhythmic movement implies primary concern for physical
       activity).

2. *Critique:*
   (a) Learner—sixth-grade science students.
   (b) Program variable—classifying selected objects.
   (c) Behavioral domain—cognitive (skill in classifying objects
       requires comprehension).

3. *Critique:*
   (a) Learner—third-grade students.
   (b) Program variable—reading comprehension skills.
   (c) Behavioral domain—cognitive (comprehension is cognitive).
4. *Critique:*
   (a) Learner—first-grade students.
   (b) Program variable—everything from the word "ability" through the remainder of the sentence.
   (c) Behavioral domain—cognitive (recall of information, comprehension, and application are primary intent).
5. *Critique:*
   (a) Learner—college students.
   (b) Program variable—appreciation, or entire sentence from the word "appreciation."
   (c) Behavioral domain—affective (appreciation is primarily affective behavior).

Chapter 4 (Allow 10 points for each evaluation statement. Exact wording not necessary. Key words should be included):

1. To develop in ninth-grade agriculture students a basic knowledge of function, composition, and properties of soil to be measured by *a written teacher-made test* on which (70% of the students correctly respond to 15 out of 28 questions). Desired level.
2. To develop the understanding ability of all foreign language students as determined by *students being able to follow and translate words in a paragraph prepared by the classroom teacher.* Minimum level.
3. To develop in students an understanding of the values which affect individual behavior and family living as measured by *a written teacher-made test* in which (80% of students are able to *list* 70% of the values previously presented in a class). Desired level.
4. To develop a better understanding of the fundamental skills in the use of tools and materials of seventh-graders as measured by *pupils using various tools or materials selected by the teacher for evaluation purposes.* Minimum level.
5. To increase the tenth-grade language arts students ability to recall the information given by panels and in group discussions as measured by *a written teacher-made test on which students can identify*

those major ideas covered by the panel or in the group discussion. Minimum level.

6. To improve the ability of seventh-grade students to compute rationale numbers as measured by *a written teacher-made test,* so that at least (51% of the students can *correctly work* 25 out of 35 *problems).* Desired level.

7. To develop the ability of seventh-grade students to measure lengths in metric system and other standards, as measured by *a written teacher-made test* in which (75% of the students measure correctly 8 out of 10 objects) using two different standards for each object. Desired level.

8. To have eighth-grade American History students recognize how the Industrial Revolution in England affected America, as determined by *a teacher-made written test on which the student can identify the appropriate changes in American society* with (51% of the students scoring 70% or better). Desired level.

9. To develop an understanding among seventh-grade social studies students that the most important differences in human behavior are learned, not inherited, as measured by *a written teacher-made test* on which (75% of the students tested scored correctly 8 out of 10 questions). Desired level.

10. To develop in eighth-grade students the ability to graph solution sets of open sentences as measured by *a 10-item teacher-made test* so that (51% of the students score 70% or better on the test.) Desired level.

Chapter 5

A. (Allow 1 point credit for each correct slash mark and for each correct E-1 and E-2 identified. Only the key words need to be italicized in the E-1 or placed in parenthesis in the E-2. E-1 and E-2 statements may overlap or include some of the same words. Exact word identification not necessary. Total points possible: 78):

1. To develop the skill of Algebra I students to evaluate scientific formulas/ as measured by *a teacher-made written test of 20 questions* such that (90% of the students can answer correctly 80% of the questions).

2. To improve accuracy of using basic mathematical skills of fifth- and sixth-grade students/ as measured by *a timed written test*

of 25 number-fact problems on which students should (complete accurately 90% of all the problems in 10 minutes).

3. To improve the performance of striking the home row keys for students taking Typing I/ so that *during a one-minute timed writing* (90% of the students will be able to type 3½ lines of home row drills without error).

4. For fifth-grade science students to gain the ability to name the parts of the eye/ as measured by their ability to *(correctly answer 80% of the questions)* on *teacher-made written examinations.*

5. To increase eighth-grade history students' knowledge of the discovery and exploration of America/ as determined by *a teacher-made written test* in which (80% of the students can *identify the important explorers and the lands that they claimed for their country* with 75% accuracy).

6. To develop the ability of eighth-grade students to change percents to decimals/ as measured by *a teacher-made written test of 20 questions* on which (75% of the students will score 80% or better).

7. To develop seventh-grade general music students' note-reading recognition/ as measured by *teacher-made tests* so that by the end of the first semester (75% of the students will be able *to read* without error) *simple rhythm patterns.*

8. To develop machine-wood safety habits in all woodworking students at BJHS/ as determined by *written teacher-made safety tests* on which (100% of the students score 85% or more).

9. To assist eleventh-grade science students in gaining a workable knowledge of and skill in writing chemical equations/ so that when given *a written teacher-made test of 20 questions* (75% of the students will score 80% or better correct answers).

10. To develop in junior high art students an awareness of van Gogh's style of painting/ so that when given *a written test involving the viewing of 25 slides, 10 of which are van Gogh's,* (90% of the students will score at least 6 out of 10 correct answers).

11. To improve the understanding of the present tense of verbs by first-year Spanish students/ as determined by *a teacher-made written test prepared from the text* being used on which (each student will achieve a minimum score of 80%).

12. To develop appreciation and understanding of Italian sixteenth-

century paintings and knowledge of paintings and artists in a high school humanities class/ to be measured by *the Rheims-Mashinga standardized art identification test* on which (all *students will* correctly *identify* 85% of the paintings).

13. To develop ability of trigonometric functions for specified arcs/ as measured by a *written teacher-made test,* with (85% of the students correctly answering 20 of 25 questions).

14. For bookkeeping students to understand the relationship of debits and credits in relation to increase and decrease in account balances/ as determined by both *teacher-prepared and standard textbook tests* on which (90% of the students score 70% or better on both tests).

15. Students in American history will get a good understanding of the first 10 Amendments to the Federal Constitution/ as measured by a *written teacher-made test,* with the expectations that (75% of students will make 75% or more).

16. To improve reading comprehension skills of students in seventh-grade special reading classes/ as determined by the *Stanford Diagnostic Reading Test, Form W, using the grade-equivalent score.* It is expected that (80% of the students will measure a gain of three grade levels by the end of the school year).

17. To improve the ability of twelfth-grade English students to punctuate sentences effectively/ so that from a *list of 50 teacher-constructed sentences,* (90% of the students will be able to punctuate correctly 45 sentences).

18. To improve the knowledge of twelfth-grade English students concerning the vocabulary of literature/ as determined by a *teacher-made written test* on which (each student must correctly define 40 out of 50 literary terms.)

19. To develop the ability of ninth-grade algebra students to identify and solve first-degree equations of one variable/ as determined by a *teacher-constructed test* on which the (majority of the students can correctly identify and solve 18 out of 20 *problems*).

20. To improve soccer skills in a ninth-grade physical education class, for a six-week unit,/ as measured by a *teacher-made skills test* with (75% of the class having a score of 85% or better).

21. To develop the ability to solve quadratic equations by Algebra II students/ as determined by (90% of the students successfully *solving* 80% of the *problems) on a teacher-made test.*

22. To improve the achievement and skill of tenth-grade students in operating a compound microscope/ as determined by *teacher observation and verbal questioning* so that after 2 hours of instruction, (90% of the students will be *able* to correctly *focus on an object using a 4 x lens, a 10 x lens, and a 40 x lens*).

23. To increase the ability of eleventh-grade English students to write effective expository paragraphs/ as measured by *their classroom writing of paragraphs using four specific methods of development according to standards set up in Warriner's Handbook*, (with 85% of the students demonstrating proficiency in writing paragraphs of definition, comparison, reasons, and details, so that ideas are communicated effectively and interestingly, according to the teacher's judgment.).

24. To increase the eighth-grade students' ability to compute with rational numbers in mathematics/ as measured by *a written objective appraisal test constructed by the classroom teacher* in which (75% of the students will answer correctly 35 out of 50 problems).

25. To increase the efficiency in shooting the jump shot of varsity basketball players/ by having *(all players) shoot the jumper from 20 feet away from the basket* and (being successful with 7 of 10 shots attempted).

26. To improve the speaking skills of seventh-grade students by increasing their vocabulary/ as determined by *teacher appraisal of a 3-minute recitation*, with (80% of the students making less than five errors in word choice).

B. (Allow 2 points credit for each correct slash mark and for each corect basic evaluation statement and for each quality criteria identified. Six points possible. Exact word identification is not essential, but key words should be included):

1. To provide instruction in language arts, math, and science that is in keeping with the interest and level of achievement of students identified as underachievers/ so that when given *written standardized tests based upon the objectives of language arts, math, and science*, there is a (positive compliance in each area with at least 90% of these objectives and a positive correlation between the student interest and achievement) as *determined by teacher observations*.

2. To develop for each grade level a program at the mathematical

maturity level of the students and emphasizing the four basic number systems with the properties of each contrasted with the other postulated systems./ Given *a written achievement test and a set of pre-established criteria for determining the adequacy of the programs' technical concerns,* (75% of the students will score 80% or above in achievement), attesting to the adequacy of the program with reference to maturity level of the students, and a *competent math authority* will find (each of the pre-established criteria correctly met), attesting to the technical excellence.

C. (Allow 6 points for correctly stated objective):
This is a creative free-response question and can be scored by the instructor or other qualified readers of the text. No credit is given for an objective that is only partly correctly stated.

Chapter 6 (Allow 5 points for each question):

(a) False	(k) True
(b) True	(l) True
(c) False	(m) False
(d) True	(n) True
(e) True	(o) True
(f) True	(p) False
(g) True	(q) False
(h) True	(r) False
(i) False	(s) True
(j) True	(t) False

Chapter 7 (Since these needs or objectives may be concerned with areas in which the students have no expertise, it is not assumed that the activities or evaluation measures will be either real or accurate. The question is more concerned with following the development process than measuring individual competencies in the area selected.)

Although the intent of this objective was to determine whether or not students could properly fill out the guideline forms, this objective also requires a certain amount of creativity on the part of each respondent. The answers provided for this chapter are just examples; they are not the specific answers to be required of the students. There are 8 possible points or sources of error in the A part and 10 possible points or sources of error in the B part of the exam. In part A the need should be filled in and parts A, B, and C of Roman numeral II should be rather specific. Any reasonable statement of a goal that includes the communication checks can serve for III-D, and any evaluation activity is acceptable for III-E. The same is true for IV-F and G. Any reasonable statement that includes the E-1 and E-2 evaluation components are acceptable. Each component part of Form A has a possibility of one error.

The same general information applies to part B of the objective. The source, type, learners, and behavioral domain should be inserted in the needs column, but only the learner and domain need to be exact or specific. Any reasonable activities, evaluation measures, and evaluation schedule is acceptable for the other columns. In the behavioral objectives the communication checks for the goal and an E-1 and E-2 must be included. Possible errors are stated on the Systems Program Planning and Development Chart, Form B.

FORM A

Optional
School Level

Optional   Optional
Subject Area   School

Optional   Optional
Page Number   Teacher

Optional
State Standard No.

BEHAVIORAL OBJECTIVE GUIDELINES

I. Delegated or Prescribed Need
   There is a need to develop more positive atti-
+1 tudes among teachers toward in-service training
   and instructional innovation.

II. Goal Statement (Communication Checks)
+1 A. Behavioral domain: Affective
+1 B. Learner: Teachers
+1 C. Program variable: Attitudes (toward specific
       variables optional)

III. Minimum Level Objective
   D. Combine A,B, and C (above) into goal statement:
+1   For teachers to improve their attitudes toward
       in-service training and instructional innova-
       tion.
   E. Identify type of evaluation or measurement in-
      strument:
+1   Semantic differential attitude scale.

IV. Desired Level Objective
   F. Combine D and E (above) into a statement:
      For teachers to improve their attitudes toward
+1   in-service training and instructional innova-
      tion as determined by a specially constructed
      semantic differential attitude scale rated
      from a -3 to a +3 point.
   G. Identify and insert the success criteria or
      standards of how well the learner must achieve
      into F (above).
      For teachers to improve their attitudes toward
+1   in-service training and instructional innova-
      tion as determined by a specially constructed
      semantic differential attitude scale rated
      ___ from -3 to a +3 points on which 75% of the
   8 teachers move at least 1 point in a positive
      direction.

FORM B

SYSTEMS PROGRAM PLANNING AND DEVELOPMENT CHART

NEEDS	GOALS	ACTIVITIES	EVALUATION MEASURES	EVALUATION SCHEDULE
The students were observed to have negative attitudes toward attending school and their perception of teachers. Source: Observed Type: Social-Emotional Learner: Students Behavioral Domain: Affective (1 error possible)	To improve student attitudes towards attending school and in perception of teachers. (1 error possible)	Utilize a "Teaching Program in Human Behavior and Mental Health" prepared by Ralph H. Ojemann et al., in the preventive psychiatry program at the University of Iowa, Iowa City. Implement course of study for grades 4, 5, and 6 including the use of textbooks for pupils, teacher's guides, and related professional materials. (1 error possible)	a. Comparison of prepost test scores and changes in the causality scores of pupils in experimental and control schools as measured by Social Causality Tests and Problems Situation Test. b. Comparison of score changes from initial to final observation in Experimental and Control Schools as recorded in observation techniques developed by Ojemann. (1 error possible)	Fall and Spring (1 point possible)

Behavioral Objective

To improve student attitudes toward attending school and in their perception of the teacher as an individual whose work is helping pupils learn as measured by a 15 % increase in the scores obtained on the Social Causality Tests and Problems Situation Test constructed by Ralph H. Ojemann.

5 errors possible (3 communication checks in goal and 2 evaluation components, E-1 and E-2)
(1) Learner = student; (2) Program variable = attitudes; (3) Implied domain = affective
E-1 = Social causality and problems situation tests (instrumentation)
E-2 = 15% increase in scores

Affective domain, 31-32
  redundancy and, 84-86

Behavior, 6, 9, 31, 35
  changes in, 93
  overt, observation of, 43
Behavioral domain, 34
  implied, 20-21, 35
  indication of, 22
  types of, 31, 35
Behavioral objective compo-
    nents, 13-25, 47, 52-53
  explanation and definition
    of, 16-17
  illustrated, 17
Behavioral objective move-
    ment, 6
Behavioral objective writers,
    major concern of, 22
Behavioral objectives, charac-
    teristics of, stated, 65
  and curriculum planning, 4,
    6
  definition of, 17
  desired level, 23-25, 52
  early articulation of, 6
  evaluation of, 4-5, 10

evaluation of goal achieve-
    ment in, 22-23
guidelines for development
    of, 78-79
minimum level, 16-19, 23-24
relating to both individuals
    and groups, 80-82
relationships to perform-
    ance objectives, 15
stating of, 7, 61-65
three levels for development
    of, 61-63
writing of, see Writing

Cognitive domain, 31-32, 35
Curriculum development, ap-
    proaches in writing for,
    82
Curriculum planning, 4

E-1, instrumentation or per-
    formance, 44
E-2, expected success level, 46
Education, quality, 4
Educational programs, 4-7
  effectiveness of, 4
  evaluation of, 4-5

literature on, 5-7
Evaluation, activities, identifi-
    cation of, 41-53
of behavioral objectives, 4-
    5, 10, 42
definition of, 5, 42, 45
of education activities, 41-53
expected success level (E-2),
    46
of goal statements, 35
instrumentation (E-1), 44
primary concerns of, 43-44
student requirement, 46-51
teacher expectancy, 46-51
Evaluation statements, basic,
    44
goals in, 47-51
optional, 45-46
precise use of words in, 77-
    78
sample, 47-51
for short-term or long-range
    results, 43-44
for specific noninstructional
    objectives, 66-71
writing of, 41-53

115

70 71 72 73   7 6 5 4 3 2 1